The Solitary Wicca Guide

THE SOLITARY WICCA GUIDE

SPELLS AND RITUALS TO PRACTICE, LEARN, AND THRIVE

ROWAN MORGANA

Illustrations by Studio Muti

ROCKRIDGE PRESS

Copyright © 2020 by Rockridge Press, Emeryville, California

No part of this publication may be reproduced, stored in a retrieval system, or transmitted in any form or by any means, electronic, mechanical, photocopying, recording, scanning, or otherwise, except as permitted under Sections 107 or 108 of the 1976 United States Copyright Act, without the prior written permission of the Publisher. Requests to the Publisher for permission should be addressed to the Permissions Department, Rockridge Press, 6005 Shellmound Street, Suite 175, Emeryville, CA 94608.

Limit of Liability/Disclaimer of Warranty: The Publisher and the author make no representations or warranties with respect to the accuracy or completeness of the contents of this work and specifically disclaim all warranties, including without limitation warranties of fitness for a particular purpose. No warranty may be created or extended by sales or promotional materials. The advice and strategies contained herein may not be suitable for every situation. This work is sold with the understanding that the Publisher is not engaged in rendering medical, legal, or other professional advice or services. If professional assistance is required, the services of a competent professional person should be sought. Neither the Publisher nor the author shall be liable for damages arising herefrom. The fact that an individual, organization, or website is referred to in this work as a citation and/or potential source of further information does not mean that the author or the Publisher endorses the information the individual, organization, or website may provide or recommendations they/it may make. Further, readers should be aware that websites listed in this work may have changed or disappeared between when this work was written and when it is read.

For general information on our other products and services or to obtain technical support, please contact our Customer Care Department within the United States at (866) 744-2665, or outside the United States at (510) 253-0500.

Rockridge Press publishes its books in a variety of electronic and print formats. Some content that appears in print may not be available in electronic books, and vice versa.

TRADEMARKS: Rockridge Press and the Rockridge Press logo are trademarks or registered trademarks of Callisto Media Inc. and/or its affiliates, in the United States and other countries, and may not be used without written permission. All other trademarks are the property of their respective owners. Rockridge Press is not associated with any product or vendor mentioned in this book.

Interior and Cover Designer: Erik Jacobsen
Art Producer: Samantha Ulban
Editor: Jesse Aylen
Production Editor: Ruth Sakata Corley

Illustrations © 2020 Studio Muti. All other images used under license © iStock and Shutterstock

ISBN: Print 978-1-64739-190-4 | eBook 978-1-64739-191-1

R1

For Silver Hazel

CONTENTS

Introduction · viii

Chapter 1: Praise Your Personal Practice · 1

Chapter 2: Awakening Your Wiccan Power · 9

Chapter 3: The Well-Stocked Solo Wiccan · 23

Chapter 4: Spells for the Solitary Wiccan · 43

Chapter 5: Wiccan Rituals for One · 83

Chapter 6: Recipes from the Solitary Kitchen · 119

Chapter 7: The Solitary Wiccan Apothecary · 157

Go Ye Happy Solitary Way · 205

Resources · 206

Glossary · 209

Spell Index · 212

Index · 214

INTRODUCTION

Welcome to *The Solitary Wicca Guide*. I have been on the Wiccan Path for more than 20 years as both a Solitary practitioner and a group member. I began as a self-taught, self-initiated Solitary Wiccan, and after a time, I joined with a core group of like-minded women.

How can I call myself a Solitary when I belong to a coven? While it might seem contradictory, the answer is quite simple: Wicca is a daily spiritual practice, not one taken up only at Esbat and Sabbat gatherings when the coven convenes. Wicca involves daily, personal, and intimate communion with the Goddess and God through prayer, offerings, and meditation; the observance of Earth's changing seasons through ritual and magick; and the celebration of waxing and waning tides as the Moon cycles from dark to new to full and back again. This daily solitary interaction helps me to create peace, balance, and wholeness in my life, while it also upholds a deeper understanding of what it truly means to be Wiccan. Issues regularly arise that require attention now rather than tomorrow or next week, when the coven will convene. Instead of waiting to employ magick, divination, or prayer to find an answer, I address the situation immediately. Although I belong to a coven, I practice my faith as a Solitary Wiccan 90 percent of the time.

Wicca is a profoundly personal journey of interaction with the natural world and the spirits that inhabit it. Daily solitary practice is my way of evolving as a Wiccan priestess. At its heart, for me, Wicca is about changing or discarding that which no longer serves your highest purpose and discovering new ways to grow and develop as an enlightened person.

You are the only one who holds the key to your spiritual awakening, and you need not look to another to provide answers. The more you practice Wicca, the more adept you will be at discovering how to be the best you can be. Study, experimentation, and faith will help you on your way. Remember, you are in control of your destiny. What is spiritually meaningful to one person may not be to another, and that's okay. The beauty of the Solitary way is that you have the freedom to choose your direction and means of travel on the Path of Wicca.

Congratulations on embracing your Wiccan Path; whether you are an experienced witch or new to the practice, this book will help you build, renew, refresh, and celebrate your Solitary way.

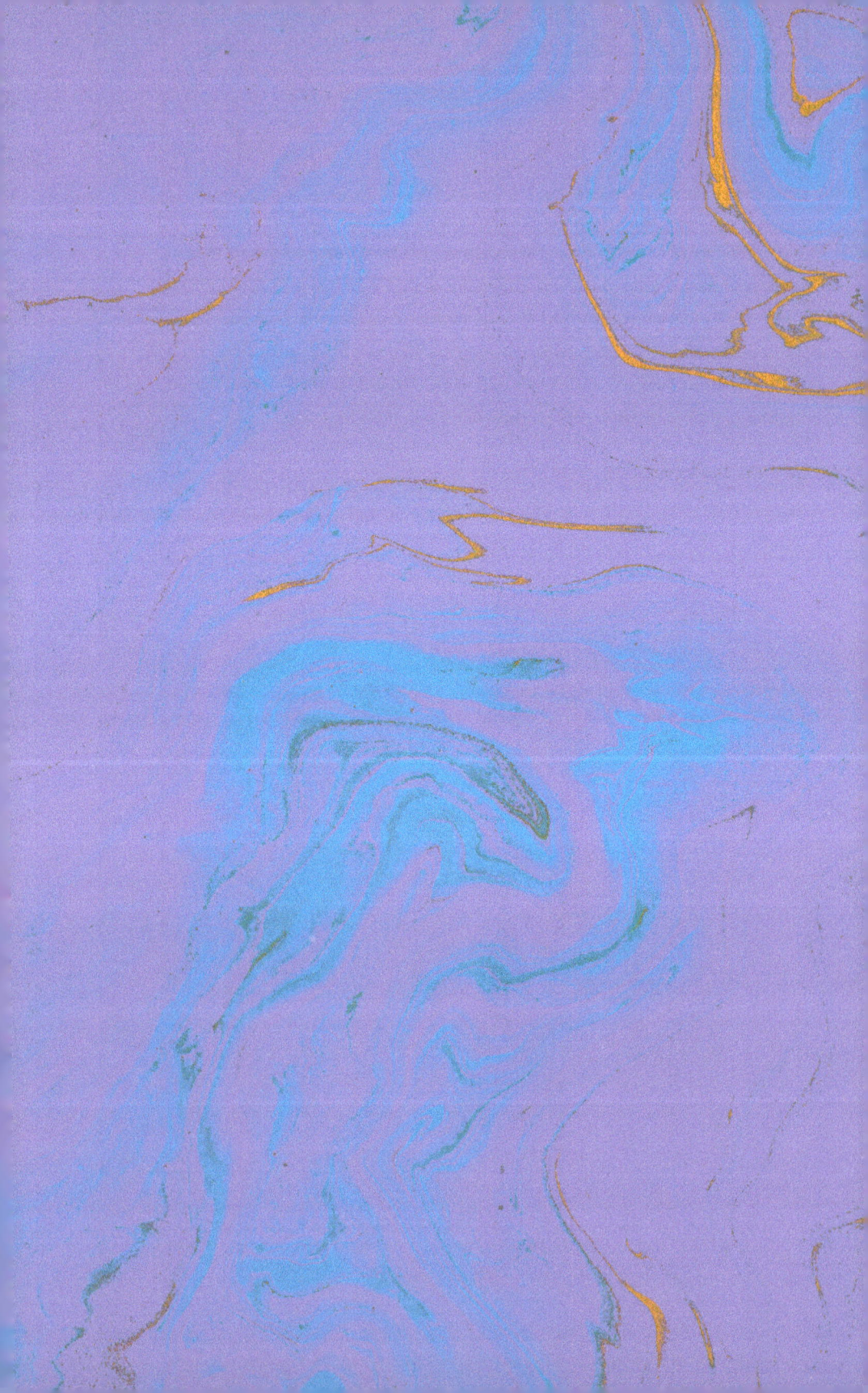

CHAPTER 1
PRAISE YOUR PERSONAL PRACTICE

This chapter explores a brief history of Wicca, the spiritual connection between Wicca and the natural world, and the benefits of the Solitary Wiccan Path. We will learn about some other Earth-based faiths and discuss their similarities and differences along with finding ways to honor nature no matter where we live.

The Roots of Belief

Wicca is a way of life that promotes peace, harmony, balance, and a reverence for all living things. It is a way of interacting with the natural world that incorporates personal integrity, spiritual and personal growth, and respect for all life. Like many Earth-centered faiths, Wicca celebrates the changing seasons and Moon phases through ritual and magick. The fluidity of Wicca allows us to incorporate aspects of other pagan paths to choose what works best for us spiritually and magickally. We can adopt the Celtic Gods if we wish, or, as with the Shamanic Path, we may use trance and meditation to connect with the spirit world. The Green tradition has a primary focus on the Earth, and as Wiccans, we revere nature, but also look outward to the Universe to draw upon its magick, energy, and mystery. The Druidic Path is arguably the origin of all Earth-based faiths, and Wiccan beliefs closely mirror Druidic practices, but we are not constrained to a particular culture.

Gerald Gardner started Wicca in the 1940s as a secretive, exclusive, and hierarchical faith. The only path to becoming Wiccan was to find a Gardnerian Coven, secure an invite, and be formally initiated into it. Wicca became a more public faith in the 1950s with the publication of Gardner's book *Witchcraft Today*, which he wrote to promote Wicca and attract new followers. The concept of Wicca caught on, and by the 1970s, many people were practicing and writing books about it. Around this time, self-initiation and Solitary Wicca became an accepted and valid way to walk the Wiccan Path.

Today Wicca is a vibrant, inclusive, and diverse religion that encourages freedom of thought and action with an emphasis on causing no harm to others.

The Singular Witch's Will

Solitary Wicca, as practiced today, is enticing to everyone who wishes to find their own spiritual path rather than follow another or a group of others. As a Solitary, you are in control of all aspects of your faith, from when to hold a ritual to what color candle you place on the altar. You decide when, where, and how you practice your faith.

You may celebrate all eight Sabbats or only those that resonate with you. You may want to honor the Moon when she is full, new, or dark, or you may wish to connect with Moon energy daily or weekly. You are the one to choose when to cast a spell and which herbs, candles, deities, chants, incantations, and prayers you will use. When you pour your soul into your spells and rituals, the effort you expend will amplify exponentially.

A note of caution: be careful not to scatter yourself in too many directions. When putting together ingredients, try not to become obsessive about getting the perfect herb or crystal. Always use your own intuition. This is especially important when you are raising magickal power. Focus and intent are the keys to effective rituals and spellcasting. As a Solitary, you may want to choose a special God or Goddess to work with and worship, or you may select many, or even none at all. You may decide to worship the Earth, Moon, stars, Universe, or whatever fills your heart with love, joy, and excitement. The door of magick is open to everyone; all you need to do is walk through it.

THE QUESTION OF ENERGY

Raising energy as a Solitary can be more complicated than building power in a group or a long-standing coven. The potential problem with raising group power, however, is that if one person is unwell or not committed to the outcome or purpose, the group energy may not complete the circuit, and the power may fizzle out. As a Solitary Wiccan, you would not bother trying to raise power for something you did not believe in or did not want to do.

To effectively build magickal power as a single person, it's essential to believe you can. You may chant, drum, spin in circles, clap your hands, dance, or use deep breathing. Be sure you concentrate on your goal, see it as accomplished, and don't allow any other thoughts to intrude on your focus. Find what works best for you and go with it.

Magick in Every Setting

As a Solitary, you may live in a city, suburb, or town or in the countryside; every environment offers opportunities to connect with nature. No matter where you are, you'll find practical ways to hone, treasure, and celebrate your craft.

THE WICCAN IN THE COUNTRY

If you live in the country, you're lucky because you have access to abundant outdoor space and privacy in which to perform your rites, spells, and rituals.

Find a natural spot: Focus on locating a natural place to conduct rites and rituals in private. It should feel sacred and resonate with you.

Craft a simple altar: Create a simple outdoor altar that incorporates the four Elements by placing a feather in the East, a votive candle in the South, a shell or dish of water in the West, and a stone or crystal in the North. You may wish to place naturally found offerings of flowers, feathers, and stones on your altar on a regular basis.

Take up wildcrafting: On your walks, you could begin wildcrafting by gathering herbs, plants, and other organic objects to use for spells and rituals. It's a good idea to get a field guide for your area so you can become familiar with your local flora.

Create a sea altar: If you're near the ocean, make shrines of driftwood, shells, twigs, and beach glass that are permanent or will be swept away with the tide. Write spells or petitions in the sand below the high-tide line, leaving them to be carried to the Gods on the enveloping waves.

Collect wild water: If you're near any natural body of water, whenever possible, use it instead of tap water for all your magickal workings.

Take it outside: What better way to honor the Full Moon than by standing in the moonlight or to celebrate the autumnal equinox than by holding your ritual in a forest of falling leaves?

Cultivate an herb garden: Grow a magickal herb garden to harvest and use in your craft.

THE WICCAN IN TOWN

If you live in the suburbs, you may have a yard with a garden you can use for outdoor rites, or access to a park, beach, or lake.

Find a spot that soothes your soul: Locate an outdoor spot that feels holy to you. Choose a spot nearby so you can spend time there frequently. There is no better way to get in touch with the divine energy of the Earth than by experiencing it.

Take your shoes off: Walking barefoot in the grass or on beach sand will immediately connect you to the natural world.

Hug a tree: Find a tree that calls to you, then sit with your back against the trunk. Imagine you have roots sinking into the Earth and branches reaching up to the sky. Once this visualization is clear, begin to see your roots releasing baneful energy into Mother Earth, where it will be transformed, and see your branches and leaves filling you with positive energy.

Make a backyard altar: Create a simple, unobtrusive outdoor altar, such as a pot filled with herbs and decorated with crystals, stones, and a pagan statue or symbol.

Collect raindrops: If you don't have access to a natural water source, collect rainwater and save it for your magick.

Buy and eat locally: Eat organic, locally sourced food whenever possible so you are consuming a direct connection to the Earth, honoring your home and neighborhood, and supporting local farmers.

THE WICCAN IN THE CITY

If you live in a city, you may not be close enough to a park or green space to visit daily, but there are still many ways to connect to nature.

Take note of nature: Walking outside and observing the sky, weather, Sun, and Moon will bring you closer to nature. Consciously feel the Earth beneath your feet. Mother Nature is tenacious and will take every opportunity to assert herself. Look for plants growing in unlikely places and honor their perseverance.

Make a list: Mentally list all the natural things you see, such as a bee, a flower, a feather, and so on. Wildcraft in the city by picking up any natural object that calls to you.

Bring it inside: Bring the outdoors indoors with potted plants, some branches or twigs in a vase, or cut flowers.

Use the Sun and Moon: During the Full Moon, place your magickal items in the moonlight to infuse them with Moon energy. On a sunny day, cleanse and charge your magickal items with Sun energy by placing them in the sunlight.

Honor the Elements: Place a representation of each Element in your home, like a vase filled with wildcrafted feathers in the East, a big red candle in the South, a bowl of water or small indoor fountain in the West, and a potted plant, stone, or crystal in the North.

No matter where you live, there is always a way for you to be part of the natural world.

The Power of Positivity

You're capable of great magick and deep connections to the Goddess and God and the natural and spiritual worlds. With power comes responsibility, and like attracts like. The Law of Attraction says you will attract into your life whatever you focus on. Many Wiccans believe in the Law of Three (or the Three-fold Law), which states that whatever energy you put into the world will be returned to you three times over. The Universe responds to both positive and negative vibrations without judgment or prejudice; it merely sends back more of the same. As a Solitary Wiccan, you must make an effort to keep your thoughts, deeds, and words in tune with what you want to attract into your life. Saying and thinking good thoughts, doing good deeds, and believing the best about yourself will bring beneficial energy your way.

Positive affirmations take command of negative thoughts through consciously repeated language. One example to combat low self-esteem is:

I am beautiful just the way I am. I love and accept myself.

Remember, positivity is key to a beneficial, healthy, and balanced Wiccan practice.

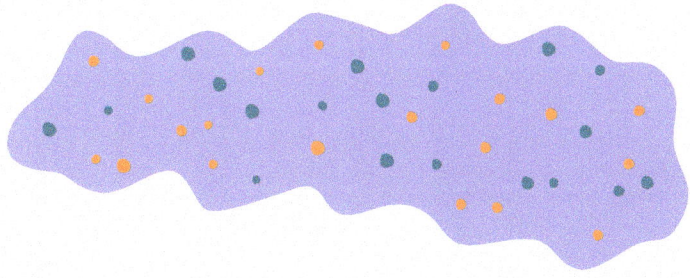

CHAPTER 2
AWAKENING YOUR WICCAN POWER

This chapter teaches you about the Wiccan Goddess and God and their place in the Solitary Wiccan path. We will talk about the different sources of magickal power that are available and explore how you can get and use them. Finally, we'll learn all about the Elements and self-initiation, including a personal self-initiation ritual.

The God for You

The Wiccan Lord and Lady may be understood as the two opposite forces found within the all-encompassing energy source, called Universal Energy or The One, which gives form and life to all existence. As humans, it can be difficult to connect emotionally with something so beyond our understanding, but through their divine balance of opposite forces, male and female, light and dark, Moon and Sun, the Goddess and God show us a way.

From winter solstice to summer solstice, the Wiccan God is the God of light and increase as the Sun grows and strengthens. From summer solstice to winter solstice, as the sun's strength begins to diminish, he is the God of darkness and decrease. While I am setting this pattern of change at the solstices, other Wiccans may choose the equinoxes or at Beltane and Samhain, the two Gaelic seasonal festivals. These methods divide the Wheel of the Year into dark and light halves; the choice of dates is open to your own interpretation.

The God of light is subdivided into two archetypes, the Hero and the Lover.

The God of darkness is subdivided into the archetypes of the King and the Sorcerer. You can understand the changing faces of both the Goddess and the God through the observation of the Wheel of the Year (page 34).

Many Wiccans choose a personal or Patron God with whom to work and interact. This relationship can create a strong bond between you and your chosen God, and you may find that you begin to communicate through dreams and visions during meditation. You may select your Patron God because he has virtues and attributes that you wish to emulate or acquire, or you may feel an affinity for a particular God. Not everyone chooses a Patron God; many Wiccans simply honor the generic Lord and Lady, or Great Father and Great Mother. The choice is entirely up to you, and you'll realize when and if your God or Goddess makes him- or herself known to you.

A simple way to connect with the God is to invoke him through heartfelt prayer and visualization of His presence near you.

The Goddess for You

The Wiccan Goddess is most often seen as three distinct entities manifested though the Maiden, Mother, and Crone.

The Maiden Goddess aspect reflects the new and waxing phases of the Moon. She is the young and independent Goddess of Spring and new beginnings. Her time of day is dawn, the time of anticipation and fresh potential. The Maiden Goddess is beautiful, artistic, and creative, and because of her youthful inexperience, she is also decisive in her actions. The Maiden Goddess is the patron of art, creativity, intelligence, and skill. She is sometimes called the virgin, but that does not mean physical virginity; it means that she is a sovereign woman, responsible for her actions, who answers only to herself. The Maiden is a skilled hunter who is a friend and companion to all young creatures.

When you witness a beautiful sunrise, spy a baby animal, walk in the forest, or see a new leaf unfurl, you are in the presence of the Maiden

Goddess. She teaches us to delight in the natural world, and her magick binds us to all that is wild and free.

The Mother Goddess aspect reflects the Full Moon. She is perhaps the most natural aspect of the Goddess to understand and recognize. Her image is that of a nurturing, protective, loving mother who is a confident adult, partner, and parent. Her season is summer, the height of the growing season, when Earth is burgeoning with life. Her color is red, the color of blood, and the life force that courses through us all. She is completion, our Mother who loves and protects the Universe and all within it. Her lessons are those of responsibility, self-discipline, and patience. The Mother Goddess teaches love of ourselves and others, and she will work to help us bring harmony and balance into our lives.

When you stand alone in the moonlight, gazing at the infinity of the stars, or swoon at the scent of a rain-washed garden, you are in the presence of the Mother Goddess.

The Crone Goddess aspect reflects the waning and dark phases of the Moon. She represents the Goddess in her character as Elder, wise woman, witch, and matriarch. Her season is winter, and her color is black, the darkness of midnight, the absorber of all light. The Crone may be the most challenging aspect of the Goddess for us to understand, for hers is the mystery of transformation, death, and rebirth, of ending cycles and completion. She is the mistress of the spirit realm, a destroyer who cuts away all that is no longer needed to make way for new growth. She teaches us spiritual completion and promises us new life when ours is over. The Crone instructs us in the art of prophecy, and she will guide us as we accept and learn the lessons given to us in this life.

Listen to her wise counsel on the darkest night of the Dark Moon as she draws near to you, whispering her deepest secrets into your soul.

Many Wiccans choose a patron Goddess who reflects the time of life they are currently experiencing. A young woman may choose a Maiden Goddess and an older woman a Crone Goddess, but regardless of your age, you are free to choose whichever Goddess calls to your heart, or none at all.

Look Back, Ye Goddesses

These goddess archetypes may be useful for help with a spell or if you wish to invite a Goddess into your sacred space. Each Goddess has specific powers that will correspond to your purpose. Remember, when you ask for something, practice reciprocity and give something, too.

Diana: Maiden Goddess of woodlands, wild animals, and the hunt. Call on Diana to help with animal magick, beauty, love, discipline, and independence. Connect with Diana during the New and Waxing Moons and the Sabbats of Imbolc, Beltane, and Ostara. Offer her fresh flowers and fruit.

Isis: Mother Goddess, who loves everyone equally no matter their station in life. Call on Isis for magickal workings that include compassion, devotion, forgiveness, grief, healing, loss, love, and sorrow. Connect with Isis at the Full Moon and the Sabbats of Litha, Lammas, and Mabon. Offer her pure water, flowers, a white feather, or a moonstone.

Hecate: Crone Goddess of magick, wisdom, and the underworld. Call on Hecate to help you increase your magickal powers and for spells concerning cycles, darkness, divination, dreamwork, nightmares, prophecy, protection, release, transformation, and witchcraft. Connect with Hecate during the Waning and Dark Moon phases and the Sabbats of Mabon and Samhain. Offer her eggs, garlic, and a croissant, or be kind to dogs.

Rhiannon: Earth Goddess of animals, change, death, justice, underworld, patience, and truth. Rhiannon appears as a lovely young woman seated upon a horse and accompanied by songbirds. Honor Rhiannon during the Sabbats of Beltane and Samhain; offer her an apple or a raven feather.

Brigid: Fire Goddess of poetry, inspiration, healing, midwifery, hearth fires, and crafts. Call on Brigid for spells and magick concerning healing, herb craft, fertility, poetry, inspiration, marriage, pregnancy, and wisdom. Connect with Brigid at Imbolc and on Sundays; offer her lit candles, ale, and coins.

Aphrodite: Water Goddess, who was born of the sea and sky as a fully grown, beautiful adult. Call on Aphrodite to aid you with attraction, beauty, and love spells, and to increase desire and fertility. Connect with Aphrodite on a Friday or at Beltane, Ostara, and Yule with offerings of frankincense and myrrh.

Flora: Air Goddess of agriculture, beginnings, fertility, growth, life, love, nurturing, rebirth, and the protection of fruit trees. Honor Flora by spending time outdoors enjoying nature, and she will bless your gardens with beauty and abundance. Offer her perfume, flowers, honey, and spring water.

Parsing Out the Powers

There are many ways to connect with the various potent powers of your Solitary craft.

PERSONAL POWER

This can also be called your inner strength or willpower. Understanding your personal power and learning how to harness it toward your desired magickal outcome is the first step to master. The most crucial aspect is concentration, the ability to focus entirely on your goal. When using visualization, try to see your goal as clearly as possible and as already manifested. Prayer, ritual, and meditation that connect you with your Higher Self will also build up your personal power.

EARTHLY OR ORGANIC POWER

This is the genuine power found within Mother Earth and her beings. You will use natural elements as magickal tools to increase the power of your intention. All things in nature have unique properties and energies called correspondences. The more you use these correspondences, the easier it is to understand their different characteristics. While there are many differing books and resources, you need to trust in your ability to feel their attributes uniquely. Remember, there is no right or wrong way; there is only what works for you.

GODDESS OR GOD DIVINE POWER

This is the universal power directly from the Goddess and God. Divine energy is present in all things; it is the life force and source that powers all of creation. You access divine power by aligning yourself with the Goddess and God through ritual, prayer, invocation, meditation, and trust. Personal power and earthly power are the vehicles that guide your magick, while divine power *is* the magick.

Embrace the Elements

Within Wicca, each of the Elements is welcomed into sacred space—sometimes specifically by name, and other times by a general greeting as an intrinsic part of casting a Circle. Once you have invoked the Elements, they protect the outer barrier of your Circle and establish a defined energy area in which you can build your magickal power. The Elements also guard the portals to the astral realms and can allow or disallow a magickal act to establish itself in the astral plane. Building a rapport with the Elements will significantly increase your magickal ability.

Each Element has its own set of traits, meanings, natural and astrological associations, and compass direction.

AIR

Traits: East, dawn, masculine, yellow, spring

Magickal Properties: activation, beginnings, communication, creativity, family, inspiration, intelligence, wisdom

Tools: athame, feather, wind instruments, pens and pencils, fan, incense

Herbs: anise, borage, dandelion, fern, hazel, lavender, mint, pine, sage, savory, star anise

Zodiac: Aquarius, Gemini, Libra

FIRE

Traits: South, noon, masculine, red, summer

Magickal Properties: courage, faith, illumination, increase, manifestation, passion, pride, purification, strength, willpower

Tools: wand, candle, matches, flint

Herbs: angelica, basil, cinquefoil, dill, heliotrope, mandrake, marigold, rosemary, tobacco, witch hazel

Zodiac: Aries, Leo, Sagittarius

WATER

Traits: West, twilight, feminine, blue, autumn

Magickal Properties: the afterlife, compassion, death, destruction, dream work, emotions, endings, love, psychic ability, visions

Tools: chalice, cauldron, trident, shells

Herbs: aster, blackberry, catnip, cowslip, eucalyptus, feverfew, heather, jasmine, poppy, rose

Zodiac: Cancer, Pisces, Scorpio

EARTH

Traits: North, midnight, feminine, green, winter

Magickal Properties: abundance, fertility, healing, the underworld, secrets, success, wealth, wisdom

Tools: pentacle disc, crystals and stones, soil, salt, sand, herbs

Herbs: barley, corn, cypress, fern, honeysuckle, mugwort, patchouli, vervain, vetiver

Zodiac: Capricorn, Taurus, Virgo

Swear to Ye Self: A Self-Dedication Ceremony

Self-dedication is a way to offer yourself to your spiritual path and formalize your commitment. Many confuse dedication with initiation, but they are different. Initiation is a formal recognition of your acceptance into a group of others. You may decide to have a self-dedication ritual immediately, or you may wait until you have studied for a year and a day, a length inspired by Celtic mythology (a year to study your craft, plus a day of contemplation). It's up to you.

Prepare yourself physically and spiritually by bathing in water infused with herbs and sea salt. Some purification herbs to consider are bay leaf, chamomile, lavender, peppermint, rosemary, thyme, and vervain.

You may wish to choose a new magickal name. Many Wiccans choose something that inspires them or has spiritual meaning, such as names of plants, animals, Goddesses and Gods, Elements, or mythological beings. Your name may be chosen for you as a gift from the Gods, come to you in a dream, be whispered in your ear, or be discovered in your soul.

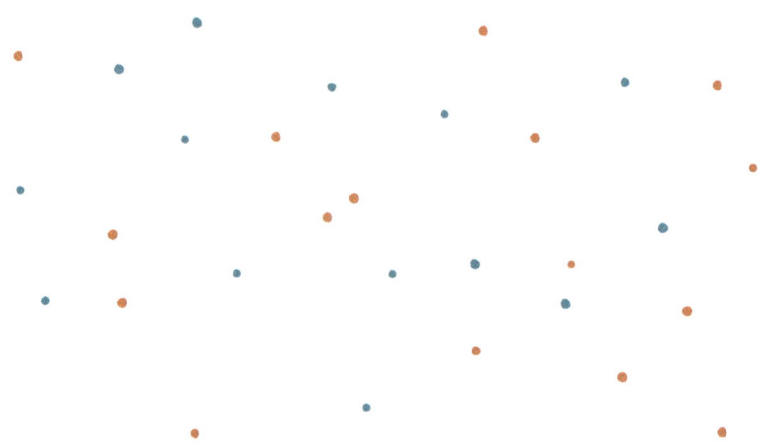

Ritual of Dedication

This ritual should be performed on the night of the New Moon within a cast Circle (page 44).

You will need:

- 8 tea light candles
- A lighter or matches
- Candle snuffer

1. Sit in the center of your Circle facing East and surround yourself with the candles at a safe distance from you. Each candle represents a Sabbat (page 35), and the Circle represents a turn of the Wheel of the Year (page 34).

2. Take a few deep breaths to ground and center yourself.

3. Light the candle directly in front of you and say:

    - *Yule—I begin anew like the newborn Sun.*

4. Light the candle to your right, then each candle in turn while speaking these incantations:

    - *Imbolc—I embrace the fires of inspiration and hope.*
    - *Ostara—I grow in spirit and faith.*
    - *Beltane—I open my heart to infinite love.*
    - *Litha—I seek the wisdom of balance.*
    - *Lammas—I honor the Earth and all Her children.*
    - *Mabon—I give thanks for all I have received.*
    - *Samhain—I accept that without endings there shall be no beginnings.*

5. Once all the candles are lit, spend a moment absorbing the magick you have created.

6. When you are ready, address the Goddess and God:

    I wish to dedicate myself to the Goddess of the Moon and stars.

    To the God of the Sun and forest, of the wild hunt and unbound nature.

    I swear to honor and uphold the cycles of the Earth and Moon

    And the Path of Wicca through study, ritual, and prayer.

    I present myself to you as [speak your name or use your new Wiccan name].

    May my rituals be filled with love, and joy, and truth.

    To praise the Goddess and to honor the God,

    I shall follow their path and grow in wisdom.

    May the Lord and Lady bless me on my magickal journey.

    So mote it be!

7. Spend some time within the enchanted space, in the presence of the Goddess and God. Listen with your heart and soul to any messages you may receive. If you are able, stay within the ring of flames until they have burned out naturally. If you cannot do so, snuff out each candle one by one, beginning with the northern candle and moving counterclockwise.

8. In your own words, thank the Goddess and God for attending your ritual.

9. Release the Circle (page 46).

Drawing Down Your Solitary Power

Everyone has magickal ability, and becoming attuned to these instinctive energies will enhance and move you toward positive personal change and growth.

But before you can effectively cast a spell, you must learn to focus your mind. As a Solitary practitioner, you're probably more free-form in your rites and rituals, which means you won't have the meditative repetition of the words, gestures, and structure of coven rituals. One of the best ways to hone your concentration and train your mind is through daily meditation. Practicing just 5 to 10 minutes a day will enhance your visualization skills, attention, and focus, all abilities crucial to successful spell casting.

A traditional Wiccan way to build up power is by hand clapping, chanting, and dancing to a rhythm or beat that slowly increases in speed. As the rhythm increases, your heartbeat and breath follow, causing the power to build up inside you. Use uncomplicated rhyming chants so you don't waste energy trying to remember them.

You can also raise power using your emotions and breath. When you feel strongly about something, your emotions cause a physical reaction. It's essential to keep a clear picture of your desire in your mind. As you visualize, take deep breaths, hold for a moment, and exhale completely.

As a Solitary, you may not always be able to rouse enough energy to power a spell on your own. The good news is that the Goddess and God will always be there to help you. All you need to do to draw on their divine energy is ask for their help using this simple ritual:

Take a few deep breaths to bring about inner peace and calm.

Face East, raise your arms high, and lift your head. Visualize a star above you filled with golden light.

See a cascade of golden light entering your body from the top of your head. Feel the light filling you with magickal energy.

Once you feel entirely full, bring your arms down and place your hands into prayer position. Bow your head and silently give thanks.

CHAPTER 3
THE WELL-STOCKED SOLO WICCAN

This chapter delves into the practical aspects of your craft. We will review the essential Wiccan ritual tools and herbs, explain how to set up an altar, and explore ritual cleansing and consecration. You will also learn about the Wiccan Sabbats and Esbats and touch on the main theme of each distinct seasonal and lunar moment.

The Tools

You'll find these tools useful in your solitary practice.

THE RITUAL KNIFE OR ATHAME

Represents the Element of Air and the power of the God. The athame is used to open and release the Magick Circle. The athame is the male portion of the Wiccan ritual called the symbolic Great Rite, which is the union of the Goddess and God created by lowering the athame into the bowl of the chalice.

CHALICE OR CUP

Represents the Element of Water and the power of the Goddess. The chalice is used to give liquid offerings and blessings. You can bless the liquid in the chalice for a magickal effect such as healing or love and then imbibe it to absorb the spell. The chalice is the female portion of the Great Rite.

CANDLES

Represent the Element of Fire and male energy. Candles are used in spells as a focal point or to burn, transform, or create change.

CRYSTALS

Represent the Element of Earth and female energy. Crystals are used as a focal point, offering, or magickal storage battery.

INCENSE

Burning incense smoke represents the Element of Air and male energy. It is used to promote ritual consciousness, as an offering, and to carry prayers, spells, and petitions into the astral realm.

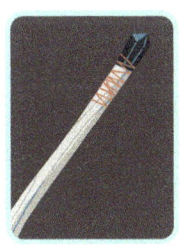

WAND

Represents the Element of Fire and is used to direct magickal energy by channeling it into the rod and then visualizing the energy beaming out from the tip.

TAROT CARDS

Are used to give insights into the future, to answer questions, and as focal points in magick spells.

RUNES

Are used for divination, and their symbols can be drawn and used in petitions, charms, and spells.

Wiccan Organics

Although there is a wealth of natural plants, herbs, and organics, here are a few of the most common and some magickal ways to use them.

PEPPERMINT

To encourage psychic dreams, drink peppermint tea before bedtime. Add peppermint in love, money, success, and protection spells. Offer peppermint to Hecate at Dark Moon.

VERVAIN

Vervain will boost the power of any magickal working. Burn dried vervain to induce visions and sprinkle it around your sacred space to purify it and protect it from negative energies.

LAVENDER

Lavender promotes visions and contact with the spirit world. To make a wish come true, place a sprig of it under your pillow. Offer lavender to the faeries, and they will befriend you. Make lavender flower tea and sprinkle it around your home to promote peace and happiness. Use lavender in spells for longevity, love, success, and sympathy.

CATNIP

Catnip relates to animal magick, friendship, happiness, and love. Pass a catnip leaf to someone to encourage a new friendship. Grow it near your door to attract good luck. Chew a leaf to bring courage and protection.

BASIL

Give basil as a housewarming gift to bring good luck. For a purifying bath, add fresh basil leaves to the water, and place it in the Ritual Chalice during initiation or dedication rites. Use basil in love and money spells.

PALO SANTO

The smoke from burning Palo Santo wood will eliminate baneful energy and create a calm, tranquil, and happy space. The beautiful scent can bring a deeper connection to the Gods and promote love, good fortune, and healing.

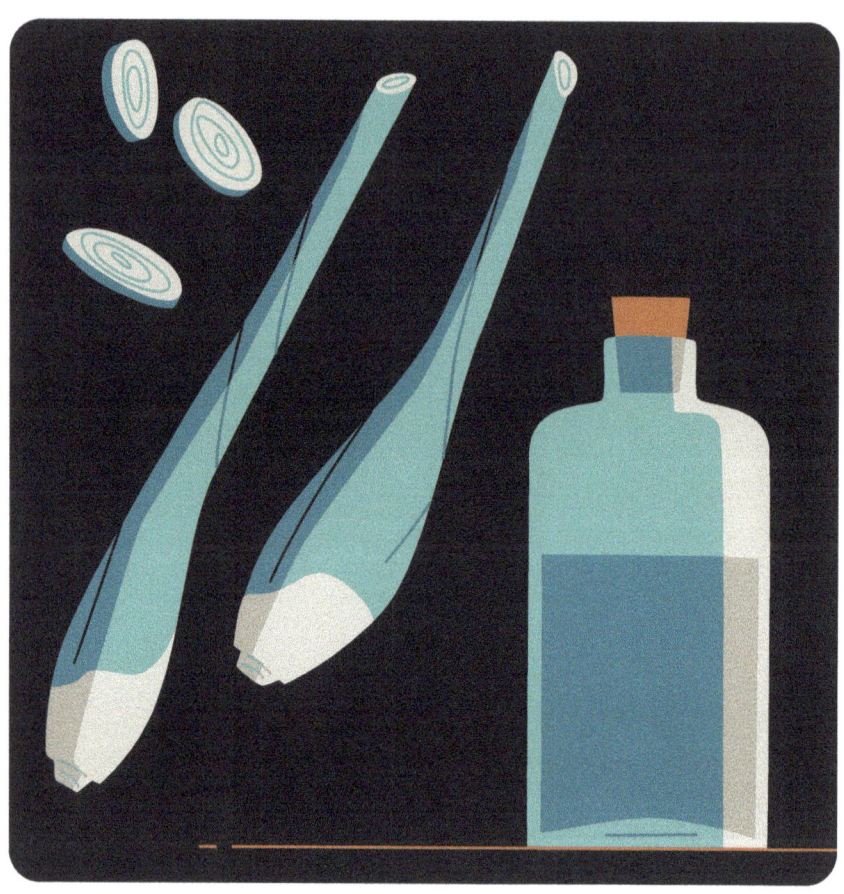

SIX ESSENTIAL OILS

These essential oils cover almost all magickal intentions:

- **Frankincense:** exorcism, spirituality, purification
- **Lemongrass:** psychic powers
- **Eucalyptus:** healing
- **Rose geranium:** protection
- **Jasmine:** love, meditation
- **Patchouli:** wealth

Setting Your Solitary Altar

Your altar is a sacred and highly personal space where you worship, make magick, and commune with your higher self. The following setup is a typical way to create a formal altar, but feel free to include items that are personally meaningful to you. Keep in mind that your altar is where the Gods are present, so treat it with respect and reverence.

RIGHT SIDE OF ALTAR

The God, Elements of Air and Fire: incense, bell, candle, wand

LEFT SIDE OF ALTAR

The Goddess, Elements of Water and Earth: chalice or cup, water, salt, cauldron

MIDDLE OF ALTAR

Spirit: pentacle, athame

FRONT OF ALTAR (FARTHEST FROM YOU)

Statue or picture of a deity, ritual focal point, candles, flowers, offering dish, seasonal elements

BACK OF ALTAR (NEAREST TO YOU)

Keep open for magickal workings

Carry Forth to Cleanse, Consecrate, and Empower

To cleanse is to remove all unwanted residual energy from an object, and to consecrate is to bless it or set it aside as something sacred. You have the power and the right of consecration because as a Wiccan, you are a priest or priestess of the Goddess and God, and their Divine force courses through your body. Cleansing and consecration are performed at the same time.

After you cleanse and consecrate, you can empower, or fill with magickal energy and intention. Knowing how to cleanse, consecrate, and empower properly is an integral part of your Solitary practice and should be done to your Wiccan tools before you use them for the first time, and periodically after that so they will always be attuned to you, both magickally and spiritually.

CLEANSING

Hold the tool in both your hands and imagine it filling with white light. When you can see that it's full of light, it is cleansed and ready for the next step.

CONSECRATION

Hold the tool up to the Gods and say:

> *This [name of tool] is dedicated to the Lord and Lady*
>
> *By my will. So mote it be!*

EMPOWERING

Hold the tool in both hands and focus your intention by having a clear picture of what you want the tool to do. Concentrate on your intention and build up power. Allow the force to grow until you can no longer contain it. Aim the energy by focusing on the tool in your hands, then release the power force into the tool.

Say:

This [name of object]

Is filled with the power to [name your intention]

By my will. So mote it be!

The Wheel of the Year

The Wiccan ritual observation of the eight Sabbats and the Moon Esbats is called the Turning of the Wheel. The Sabbats celebrate the changing seasons and the evolving relationship between the Goddess and God throughout the year.

An Esbat is a ritual that happens during the night of the Full Moon. Its purpose is to celebrate the Moon, honor the Goddess, and take advantage of heightened Moon power by casting spells. There are 13 Full Moons each year, and each one has a different tide.

While the following pages explore the Wheel of the Year along with each monthly moon, the 13th moon is known as the Blue Moon. These are rarer, falling when there are two Full Moons within a month's time, and the second is called Blue. Interpretations can vary, but these elusive Blue Moons have been associated with increased awareness and sensitivity, magickal potency, and time to grow one's magickal knowledge.

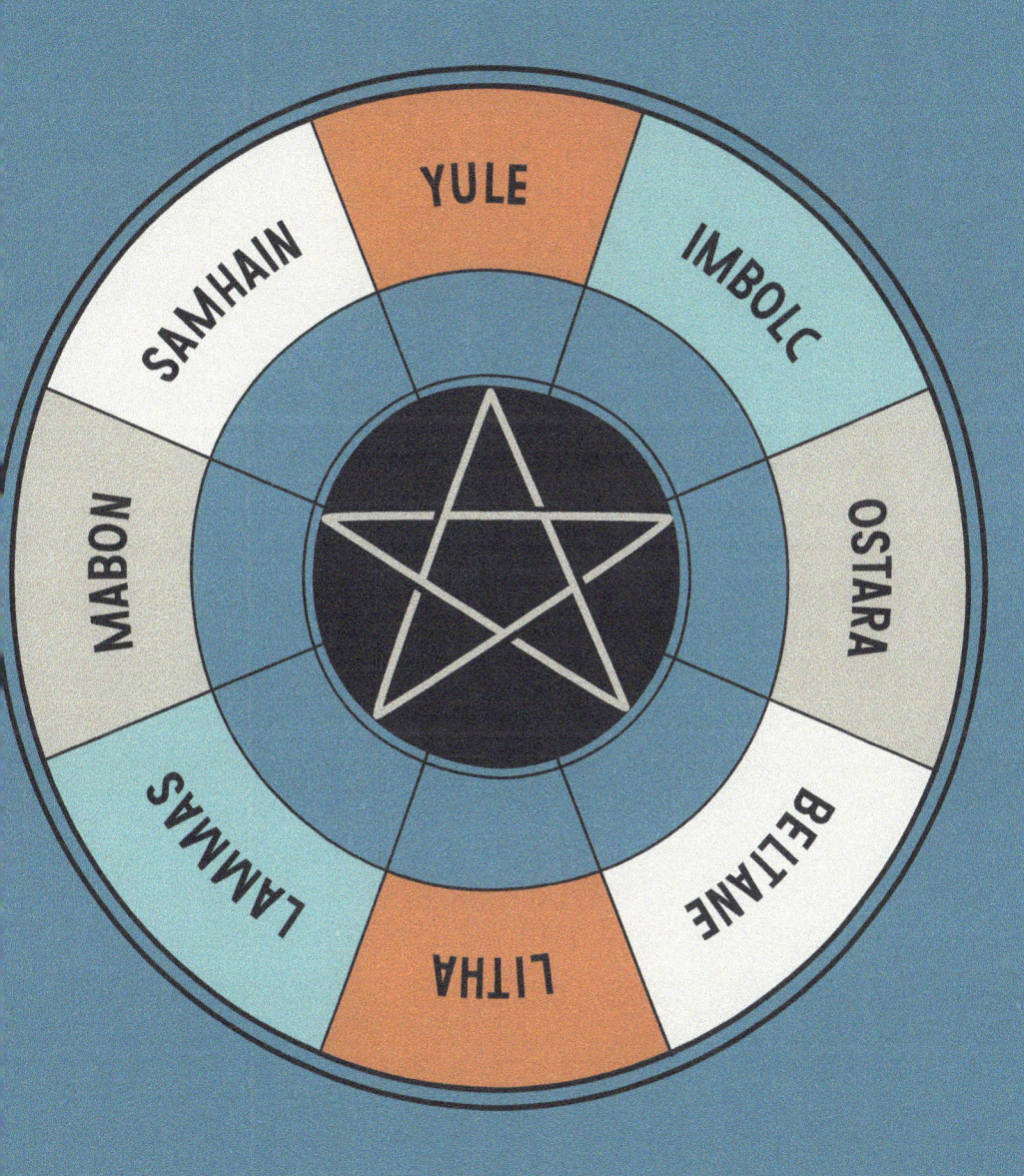

THE SABBATS

From Yule to Samhain, let's explore the truly powerful Sabbats of the year.

Yule (Winter Solstice): December 20–23
- The longest night of the year is celebrated with hope and faith because from this day forward, the daylight will increase as the Wheel turns toward the light. The Goddess returns from the Underworld and gives birth to the Sun King.

Imbolc (Candlemas): February 2
- Daylight is increasing, and the Goddess and God are presented as young and innocent children who have not yet come into their power. It is a celebration of anticipation and planning for the future through meditation, purification, and rededication to your spiritual path.

Ostara (Vernal Equinox): March 19–22
- Night and day are balanced, the days are longer, and the Earth has awakened from her long winter's sleep. The Goddess and God have grown into young and virginal lovers who dance hand in hand across the land. Wherever their feet touch the Earth, blooming flowers appear. It is a celebration of Mother Earth, new life, promise, and joy.

Beltane: May 1
- The Goddess and God have grown into adults; they become lovers and marry. Their union signals the beginning of Earth's growing cycle. It is a lighthearted celebration of fertility, love, sex, passion, harmony, and happiness.

Litha (Summer Solstice): June 20–22

- The longest day of the year is tinged with sadness because from this day forward, the sunlight will begin to decrease as the Wheel turns toward the darkness. The Goddess and God are at the height of their power as they rule over the ripening crops.

Lammas (Lughnasadh): August 1

- The sunlight is steadily decreasing and the nights are getting cooler, signaling the beginning of fall. It is a celebration of the first harvest and of honoring grain as the earthly embodiment of the joint powers of the Goddess and God.

Mabon (Autumn Equinox): September 21–24

- Night and day are balanced; the Goddess has aged into her aspect as Crone and the old God has begun his journey into the Underworld. It is a celebration of the second harvest and the end of the growing cycle.

Samhain: October 31

- At Samhain the God dies and the grieving Goddess follows him into the Underworld, causing the veil to thin between the living and the dead. Samhain is a traditional time to communicate with the spirit world and to honor lost loved ones, ancestors, and guides.

THE MOON ESBATS

Within each Esbat, you'll find a new wave of Wiccan purpose and magickal inspiration, as each moon carries its own distinctive energies.

COLD MOON — **JANUARY**
The tide of new beginnings

QUICKENING MOON — **FEBRUARY**
The tide of preparation and purification

STORM MOON — **MARCH**
The tide of hope, growth, and prosperity

WIND MOON

APRIL

The tide of confidence, friendship, and healing

FLOWER MOON

MAY

The tide of creativity, love, and fertility

STRONG SUN MOON

JUNE

The tide of transition, preparation, and releasing

The Well-Stocked Solo Wiccan

JULY

The tide of peace, protection, and justice

AUGUST

The tide of harvest, abundance, and gratitude

SEPTEMBER

The tide of balance, cleansing, and protection

OCTOBER

The tide of meditation, courage, and healing

NOVEMBER

The tide of grounding, preparation, and transformation

DECEMBER

The tide of endings, endurance, and rebirth

CHAPTER 4
SPELLS FOR THE SOLITARY WICCAN

Now that we have learned about cleansing, consecration, and empowerment and considered how to mark the Wiccan year, we will launch into spells tailored just for you, the Solitary Wiccan. We begin by learning how to cast and release a Magick Circle, then go on to a selection of spells designed to bring positive changes to your personal and magickal lives.

Cast Your Singular Circle

Learning to cast a Magick Circle before attempting magick is essential. A correctly cast Circle will prevent harmful energy from entering and will amplify and contain your personal power and the energy that you raise. While you are actively casting the Circle, visualize it as clearly as possible.

You will need:

- Four white votive or tea light candles or:
    - 1 yellow candle for East
    - 1 red candle for South
    - 1 blue candle for West
    - 1 green candle for North
- A small container of water with a pinch of salt added
- Incense of your choice
- A lighter or matches
- Candle snuffer
- Athame or wand (or use the index and middle fingers of your power hand)

1. If possible, place your altar in the center of the area where you will be casting the Circle. Place the four candles at each corresponding quadrant: East, South, West, and North.

2. Calm and center yourself. Silently or aloud, ask the Goddess and God to be present and to bless you.

3. Beginning and ending in the East, using your athame, wand, or finger, begin to cast the Circle by walking clockwise three times around the outer perimeter of your Circle while visualizing a sphere of light completely surrounding you—around, above, and below. Once you are finished, say: *By my will, I cast the Magick Circle.*

4. Beginning and ending in the East, walk around the perimeter of the Circle three times while sprinkling the salted water. When you are finished, say: *By Earth and Water, this Circle is bound!*

5. Light the incense. Beginning and ending in the East, walk around the perimeter of the Circle three times while wafting the incense smoke. When you are finished, say: *By Fire and Air, this Circle is bound!*

Cast Your Circle

6. Light the Eastern candle and say: *I invite the Element of Air to join me in my rite! Merry meet!*

7. Light the Southern candle and say: *I invite the Element of Fire to join me in my rite! Merry meet!*

8. Light the Western candle and say: *I invite the Element of Water to join me in my rite! Merry meet!*

9. Light the Northern candle and say: *I invite the Element of Earth to join me in my rite! Merry meet!*

10. When all the candles are lit, stand in the center of the Circle with arms outstretched and say: *The Circle is cast. Blessed be!*

11. Begin your magickal work.

Spells for the Solitary Wiccan

Release Your Singular Circle

Once you have finished your ritual or magick spell, you must release the Circle to dissipate the force you created. Once your Circle has been released, all the residual energy you raised will dissipate harmlessly into the universe.

You will need:

- A candle snuffer (or use the tip of your athame)

1. In the North, snuff out the candle and say: *I thank the Element of Earth for attending my rite. Merry part.*

2. In the West, snuff out the candle and say: *I thank the Element of Water for attending my rite. Merry part.*

3. In the South, snuff out the candle and say: *I thank the Element of Fire for attending my rite. Merry part.*

4. In the East, snuff out the candle and say: *I thank the Element of Air for attending my rite. Merry part.*

Release Your Circle

5. Beginning and ending in the North, with your athame, wand, or finger pointed toward the perimeter of the Circle, release it by walking counterclockwise once around the outer edge. Visualize the sphere of light breaking apart and dispersing into the atmosphere. Know in your heart that the magick you have created is complete and the Circle is released. Say: *The Circle is released, by my will. So mote it be!*

Simple Solitary Wiccan Spells

Now it's time to make a little magick. Using your willpower, intention, and faith—anything can happen!

Following the Path Honey Jar Spell

To strengthen your commitment, make this honey jar using herbs, crystals, and incense chosen to infuse the jar with your intention. The honey binds it all together with sweetness and light!

You will need:

- Sandalwood incense
- A lighter or matches
- Candle snuffer
- A resealable glass jar or bottle
- A small piece of parchment paper
- A felt-tip pen
- Small clear and rose quartz crystals
- Lemon balm
- Peppermint
- Rosemary
- Sage
- Thyme
- A small dish of pure honey
- A small charm strung on a white ribbon
- A small white candle

1. On the night of the Full Moon, gather all the ingredients and cast your Circle (page 44).

continued ▶

Following the Path Honey Jar Spell *continued*

2. Cleanse, consecrate, and empower the jar, crystals, herbs, honey, charm, and candle (page 32).

3. Light the incense, then hold the open end of the jar over the smoke, allowing it to fill the bottle. Place it to one side.

4. Write your name on the paper and add a few words on your intention, then use the pen to draw an Earth-invoking Pentagram on top of your words to bind them:

Earth-invoking Pentagram

5. Hold the paper over the incense smoke and chant three times:

Honey jar of sweet delight,

My intent is set this Full Moon night!

6. Fold the paper twice, then place it at the bottom of the jar.

7. Smudge the crystals and herbs in the smoke, then place them in the jar.

8. Pour the honey into the jar while chanting:

The path of Wicca I shall bide,

God and Goddess shall be my guides!

9. Place the lid on the jar, then tie the ribbon and charm around it.

10. Using a lighter or match, carefully melt the bottom of the candle until it begins to drip onto the jar lid. Affix the candle to it. Light the candle, and visualize your Solitary life.

11. When ready, snuff out the candle and release your Circle (page 46). Place the jar in a prominent place to remind you of your commitment.

Spell to Strengthen Magickal Power

You will need:

- 2 black candles and candleholders
- A candle-carving tool (a nut-pick, pushpin, or metal skewer works well)
- Patchouli essential oil
- An amber or obsidian crystal
- A lighter or matches
- Candle snuffer
- Frankincense incense
- Parchment paper
- Pen

1. Cast this spell on a Friday or Monday when the Moon is waxing to take advantage of the Moon tide of increase.

2. Cast your Circle (page 44) and cleanse, consecrate, and empower the candles, essential oil, and crystal (page 32). Carve the candles with Triple Moon symbols and anoint them with the essential oil. Anoint your hands, heart, and brow.

Triple Moon

3. Place the candles in holders in front of you and set the crystal between them. Light the candles and say:

Element of Fire, I call on you to ignite the power of magick within me.

continued ▶

Spell to Strengthen Magickal Power *continued*

4. Light the incense and draw the smoke toward you with both hands. Breathe deeply, relax, and begin to envision yourself filled with limitless magickal potential. Allow your body to sway, gently and slowly, as you see yourself filling with magick power. Take your time with this; keep up the visualization until you feel full.

5. When you are ready, take up the parchment and pen and sketch yourself as the witch you want to be. You may also add words, symbols, or pictures—whatever feels right. When you're finished, place the paper between the two candles.

6. Pick up the crystal, hold it to your Heart Chakra, and visualize magick power flowing into it. When you feel that the stone is full, use your finger to draw an Earth-invoking Pentagram over it to seal the charge.

7. Place the crystal between the candles. While gazing at the tableau, repeat the following incantation three times three (nine times in total). While you are chanting, allow your words to flow in rhythm as you sway gently from side to side.

Earth-invoking Pentagram

I draw the magick

the magick is me

The magick shall be

Magick in me

I will myself

I am the spell

The magick is me

I shall be

The magick inside

Magick flows

I receive

World of magick

Goddess and God

Moon and Sun

The power grows

The magick is me

And I will be!

8. If you can, allow the candles to burn down naturally. Otherwise, snuff the candles.

9. Release your Circle (page 46).

10. Place the parchment and crystal on your altar or in a place of prominence where you will see them daily.

11. Whenever you feel the need for increased magickal power, hold the crystal to your Heart Chakra and chant:

Moon and Sun

The power grows

The magick is me

And I will be!

New Moon Out with the Old, In with the New Spell

This spell will banish negative energy and bring in positive energy. It's best done on the night of the New Moon to take advantage of the Moon tide of growth and new beginnings.

You will need:

- 1 black candle, for banishing, placed on the left of the altar in a holder
- A lighter or matches
- Candle snuffer
- 2 small squares of parchment paper
- Black and blue pens
- Lavender oil, for banishing
- A heatproof container or cauldron
- 1 white candle, for attraction, placed on the right of the altar in a holder
- Frankincense essential oil, for blessing

1. Cast your Circle (page 44). Cleanse, consecrate, and empower the candles and essential oils (page 32).

2. Light the black candle and say:

    I allow all that does not serve my highest good to peacefully leave my life. I will it so.

3. On one piece of parchment, using the black pen, write your negative feelings and thoughts. Don't hold back; let your emotions bleed into your written words. When you are ready, sprinkle nine drops of the lavender essential oil over the paper, then light it in the flame of the black candle and place in the heatproof dish. As it is burning, chant three times:

All that is baneful shall now depart,

I free my body, soul, and heart.

4. Snuff out the black candle.

5. Light the white candle and say:

   I allow all that serves my highest good to enter my life peacefully. I will it so.

6. Using the blue pen on the remaining parchment, draw the Star Sigil (for wishes, luck, good fortune, inspiration, and freedom).

7. Write your name several times in a circle surrounding the star. Sprinkle nine drops of the frankincense essential oil over the paper. Light it in the flame of the white candle and place it in the heatproof dish. As it is burning, chant three times:

Star Sigil

My heart and soul filled with the light,

Of positive energy this New Moon night!

8. Spend a few moments basking in the positive energy you have created with your magickal will.

9. When you're ready, snuff out the white candle and release your Circle (page 46).

10. Take the container of ashes outdoors and cast them into the wind so the winds of change may carry them away.

Spells for the Solitary Wiccan

Self-Love Affirmation Spell

This spell will help you learn to love and accept yourself just the way you are. It is best performed on a Friday, the day of Venus.

You will need:

- A red candle and candleholder
- Rose or rose geranium essential oil
- A lighter or matches
- Candle snuffer
- A large mirror positioned on the altar so you can see your reflection
- A palo santo or incense stick
- A picture of yourself
- A large red paper heart

1. Cast your Circle (page 44). Cleanse, consecrate, and empower the candle, essential oil, mirror, picture, and paper heart (page 32).

2. Anoint the candle with the essential oil, place it in the holder, light it, and place it directly in front of the mirror.

3. Look in the mirror and see the perfection that is unique to you. If a negative thought about yourself comes into your mind, don't ignore it. Instead, tell yourself you are the living embodiment of the Goddess and God, they are within you, and their spark of light will shine through if you allow it.

4. Light the palo santo or incense and waft its smoke over your entire body. Visualize the smoke drawing out all the negative thoughts that have blocked your quest for self-acceptance and love. Visualize all your old fears and doubts drifting away with the rising smoke.

5. Place your picture on top of the paper heart. Their union symbolizes your commitment to love and accept yourself. Allow your heart to fill with love, then move on to the next step.

6. Anoint your hands, heart, and brow with the essential oil while chanting this affirmation seven times:

I love myself exactly as I am.

I love my body exactly as it is.

I love my mind exactly as it is.

I love my spirit exactly as it is.

Blessed be the God/dess within me.

7. Snuff out the candle and release your Circle (page 46). For the next seven days, place a dab of rose essential oil at your Heart Chakra and repeat the affirmation seven times. The scent of the oil and the chanting will remind you to love yourself wholly and unconditionally.

Spell to Draw Like-Minded People

Whether you meet virtually or in person, this spell is designed to attract others, enabling a sense of community. Begin it seven days before the Full Moon.

You will need:

- A blue seven-knob candle, for obtaining wishes
- A candle-carving tool
- Candleholder
- Attraction Oil (pour ¼ ounce sweet almond or grapeseed oil into a small glass vial, add 20 drops of vanilla essential oil, and cap the vial)
- A lighter or matches
- Candle snuffer
- Dried jasmine, lavender, and catnip
- Mortar and pestle
- 6-inch square of blue or gold cloth
- A small clear quartz crystal
- 6-inch piece of blue or gold ribbon

1. Cast your Circle (page 44). Cleanse, consecrate, and empower the candle, Attraction Oil herbs, and crystal (page 32).
2. Beginning at the top knob of the candle, carve the words "Friendship, Witchcraft, Wicca."
3. On the second knob, carve your name and the sigil for Friendship, Witchcraft, Wicca.
4. On the third knob, carve the date and Friendship sigil.
5. On the fourth knob, carve the Rings rune (to strengthen relationships) and Friendship sigil.
6. On the fifth knob, carve the Sun rune (for growth and happiness) and Friendship sigil.

Friendship, Witchcraft, Wicca Sigil

Rings Rune

Sun Rune

Moon Rune

Water-invoking Pentagram

7. On the sixth knob, carve the Moon rune (for magick, change, secrets, and transitions) and Friendship sigil.

8. On the seventh knob, carve a Water-invoking Pentagram (to bind the magick with love) and Friendship sigil.

9. Anoint the candle with the Attraction Oil, taking care to begin at the top of the candle and rotate it clockwise.

10. Put the candle in the holder and light it. While the first knob of the candle is burning, place the herbs and seven drops of Attraction Oil into the mortar and begin crushing them with the pestle while chanting seven times:

Herbs and oil and candle fire,

Bring to me my desire.

continued ▶

Spell to Draw Like-Minded People *continued*

11. Carefully pour the herbs into the center of the cloth. Anoint the crystal with seven drops of Attraction Oil and place it on top of the herbs. Tie the bag shut with the ribbon and hold it to your Heart Chakra. Empower the sachet with thoughts of friendships with Wiccan camaraderie, magick, and wisdom. Concentrate strongly for as long as you can; ideally, you will continue until the first knob of the candle has melted.

12. Once the first knob has burned, snuff out the candle and place the sachet near it. Release your Circle (page 46).

13. Empower the sachet and burn one knob of the candle every night until the candle is gone, ending on the night of the Full Moon. Keep the sachet in a safe place or on your altar as a friendship talisman.

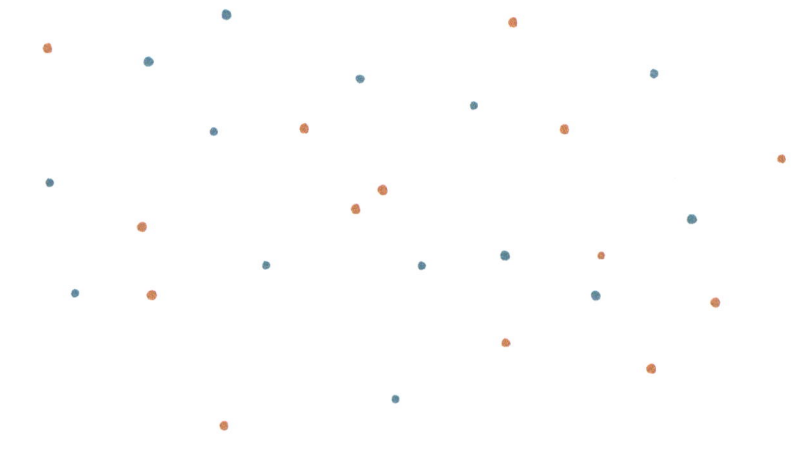

Hecate's Key Spell

This spell will help attune you to the wisdom and power of the Crone Goddess by enchanting a key. Keys are a symbol sacred to Hecate, and from the beautiful skeleton key to mundane house key, all have the power to lock and unlock, to open and close. Cast this spell on the night of the Dark Moon—Hecate's Moon.

You will need:

- 3 black candles and candleholders
- A lighter or matches
- Candle snuffer
- Myrrh incense
- 3 moonstone crystals
- 3 fresh sprigs of yew, hazel, or willow
- Mugwort or lavender
- A skeleton key on a black ribbon long enough to hang around your neck
- A small dish of water with a dash of salt stirred in

1. Cast your Circle (page 44). Cleanse, consecrate, and empower the candles, incense, crystals, herbs, and key (page 32).

2. Light the candles and say:

   Dark Crone Goddess Hecate,

   Descend to me, please join my rite.

3. Light the incense and say:

   I offer your sacred incense,

   Descend to me, please join my rite.

continued ▶

Hecate's Key Spell *continued*

4. Place a crystal in front of each of the candles and say:

   I offer your sacred crystals,

   Descend to me, please join my rite.

5. Place a sprig of yew (or hazel or willow) in front of each candle and say:

   I offer your sacred yew [hazel or willow].

   Descend to me, please join my rite.

6. Sprinkle a circle of mugwort or lavender around the candles, incense, crystals, and sprigs and say:

   I offer your sacred herb.

   Descend to me, please join my rite.

   Dark Crone Goddess,

   Wise and Elder One,

   Teach me the deep mysteries

   Of your Ancient Heka Magick

   Guide and protect me,

   As I learn your ways.

7. Pick up the key and say:

   I dedicate this key to Hecate; may it unlock wisdom.

8. Pass the key through the incense smoke and say:

   Hecate's smoke shall fill this key

   With the knowledge of eternity.

9. Pass the key through the candle flames and say:

   Hecate's fire shall fill this key

   And burn away negativity.

10. Dip the key into the bowl of water and say:

    Hecate's water shall fill this key

    With magick, dreams, and prophecy.

11. Place the key upon each crystal in turn and say:

    Hecate's stones shall fill this key

    With her wisdom and authority.

12. Hold the key in both of your hands and visualize the silver light of Hecate filling the key. Keep up the visualization until you feel the key is full.

13. When you are ready, thank Hecate, snuff out the candles, and release your Circle (page 46).

14. To use the key in rituals and spells, turn it to the right to open and draw energy, or turn it to the left to close and banish energy.

15. Take the candle stubs, crystals, sprigs, and herbs to a place where three roads or paths cross and leave them there. Crossroads are sacred to Hecate. If there are no crossroads near you, bury the ingredients in the Earth or simply leave them outside to compost.

Cleansing Bath for Purification

Turn your bath into a sea of magick with a few drops of essential oils, some herbs, and crystals. Whether you're having a bad day or indulging a bad habit, take a purifying, cleansing bath and banish it.

You will need:

- A handful of Epsom salts
- Fresh oak leaves, if available
- Heliotrope flowers, fresh or dried
- Mint or rosemary, fresh or dried
- An amethyst crystal
- Olive oil
- Lavender essential oil

1. Fill your bathtub with warm water and add the Epsom salts, oak leaves, heliotrope, mint or rosemary, the crystal, a few drops of olive oil, and a few drops of essential oil.

2. Immerse yourself in the warm waters and cast a Circle of protection, envisioning a sphere of white light surrounding you.

3. Take three deep breaths, close your eyes, and focus on the scent of the herbs and oils, feel the bathwater drawing out all negative energy through every pore of your body, purifying and recycling it through the scented waters.

4. When you feel clean, release the Circle by visualizing it thinning and disappearing like a soap bubble.

5. You may wish to cleanse your bathtub to remove any residual negative energy.

A Solitary Spell for Self-Healing

This healing spell should be used in conjunction with treatments prescribed by your medical practitioner. Cast this spell on the night of the Full Moon.

You will need:

- An indigo candle and candleholder
- A candle-carving tool
- Lavender essential oil
- A lighter or matches
- Candle snuffer
- A picture of yourself
- Magick Wand (or use the index and middle finger of your power hand)
- A crystal bowl of pure water with one drop of blue food coloring added
- A fresh sprig of cedar, lavender, cowslip, fennel, or sage
- A bouquet of fresh flowers, for an offering

1. Cast your Circle (page 44). Cleanse, consecrate, and empower the candle, essential oil, and herb sprig (page 32).
2. Carve your name and astrological symbol on the candle and anoint it with the essential oil.
3. Place it in the candleholder, light it, and put your picture in front of it.
4. Chant three times,

   Lord and Lady, I ask of thee

   Enter my Circle be here with me.

   Please aid me in my healing rite,

   I honor you this blessed night.

continued ▶

A Solitary Spell for Self-Healing *continued*

5. Take a moment to feel the presence of the Lady and Lord.

6. Pick up your Magick Wand and envision yourself surrounded by a circle of sparkling, healing blue light. Allow the light to fill your body. Using your will, direct the light into the wand. Envision the wand filled with blue light, then see the light begin to flow out of the wand's tip. Point the wand toward your picture and see the shimmering blue light surround it.

7. In your mind's eye, see yourself completely healthy and free of all illness. Concentrate on this vision for as long as you can.

8. When you are ready, wave your wand back and forth, allowing the residual healing energy to flow out and away into the universe. Once all the energy has dissipated, place your wand on the altar.

9. Put the blue water in front of you and pick up the plant sprig. Dip it into the water and use it to draw an Earth-invoking Pentagram over your picture to seal the charge.

10. Dip the sprig into the water once again and use it to draw a Pentagram on your body and say:

    Touch your forehead, then left knee

    From left knee to right shoulder

    From right shoulder to left shoulder

    From left shoulder to right knee

    From right knee to forehead

Earth-invoking Pentagram

11. Present the offering of flowers to the Lord and Lady while chanting three times:

   Goddess and God of healing blue,

   Accept this gift I offer you.

   I thank you for your help tonight,

   You shared your gift of healing light.

12. Snuff out the candle and release your Circle (page 46).

New Moon Letters to the Goddess

Cast this spell during the New Moon to reflect on the past lunar cycle and to set your intentions for the new lunar cycle.

You will need:

- 3 white candles and candleholders
- Sandalwood incense
- A lighter or matches
- Candle snuffer
- 3 pieces of paper and a pen
- 3 white flowers, such as roses, lilies, or tulips
- A cauldron or heatproof container

1. Cast your Circle (page 44). Place the three white candles in a semicircle in front of you and light the incense.

2. Invite the Goddess into your sacred space, saying:

   Maiden Goddess Diana

   Of the Silver Bow,

   I invite you into my Circle

   On this night of the New Moon.

   Blessed be!

3. Light the candle on the left and begin to write your first letter to the Goddess. Your message could start by saying, "Dear Goddess," and could be written as if speaking to a friend. Write down everything that you are grateful for, including all the spiritual gifts you have received during the past Moon cycle. When you're finished, place your first floral offering, one of the white flowers, in front of the lit candle and say:

Thank you, Diana, New Moon Goddess,

I am grateful for all that I have received.

4. Fold the note and tuck it under the first burning candle.

5. Light the middle candle and write your second letter to the Goddess. Write down everything that did not go so well over the past Moon cycle, including mistakes and errors in judgment that you are not proud of. Take responsibility for your actions and forgive yourself. When you're finished, place your second floral offering in front of the candle and say:

Diana, New Moon Goddess,

Help me to banish all that is not for my highest good.

6. Burn the note in the cauldron to release all residual negative energy into the Universe.

7. Light the last candle and take time to consider what you would like to manifest during the coming Moon cycle. When you are ready, write down everything you want to accomplish magickally, physically, spiritually, and personally. When you're finished, place your third floral offering in front of the candle and offer it to Diana as a sacred petition:

Diana, Goddess of the New Moon,

I have reflected and am grateful,

I have acknowledged and accepted,

I have been cleansed and made ready,

continued ▶

New Moon Letters to the Goddess *continued*

Bless these words and my intentions,

May your love guide me.

So mote it be!

8. Keep the note on your altar until the next New Moon, when you may wish to reread it as a reference for the next Moon cycle.

9. Take a few moments to bask in the magick you have wrought with the help of the Goddess. When you are ready, snuff out the candles and release your Circle (page 46).

The Crystal Pentagram Spell

This spell will help you create an added source of power and protection using crystals placed in the form of a Pentagram. Cast this spell on a night of the Waxing Moon to take advantage of the drawing and increasing Moon tide.

You will need:

- 5 clear quartz crystals
- A small bowl of salted water
- A compass
- A small bowl of fresh water
- A soft towel

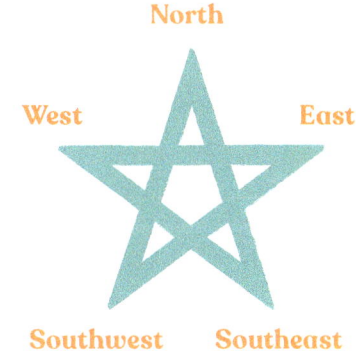

1. Perform this spell in the room or sacred space where you will most frequently practice magick. Before you begin, place the crystals in the bowl of salted water to gently cleanse them. While the stones are soaking, use the compass to find the directions of North, East, Southeast, Southwest, and West.

2. Remove the crystals from the salt water and place them in the bowl of fresh water for a few moments, then dry them thoroughly with the towel. Your stones are now ready to be charged with your intention.

continued ▶

The Crystal Pentagram Spell *continued*

3. Hold the crystals to your Heart Chakra and imagine them as batteries of stored energy for you to use whenever you need extra power. Hold this visualization for as long as you can. When you're ready, begin to place the crystals.

   - Place a crystal in the North and say: *Element of Earth, I ask that you ground and stabilize my spells of magick.*

   - Go to the Southwest, place a crystal, and say: *Elements of Fire and Water, I ask that you strengthen the currents of my magickal energy.*

   - Go to the East, place a crystal, and say: *Element of Air, I ask that you ignite my spells with the flames of creativity.*

   - Go to the West, place a crystal, and say: *Element of Water, I ask that you grant a deep understanding of the mysteries of witchcraft.*

   - Go to the Southeast, place a crystal, and say: *Elements of Fire and Air, I ask that you fan the fires of communication and passion.*

   - Walk back to the North and say: *The Pentagram is complete!*

5. Stand in the center of the Pentagram crystal grid and visualize streams of light connecting the crystals to one another to form a glowing star. See the light grow and expand until you are completely surrounded. Whenever you raise energy, your crystals will absorb and retain some of it for later use. When you need extra magickal power, stand in the center of the Pentagram grid and visualize it awakening and connecting to you through the energy of light.

Prosperity Meditation Spell

This meditation will draw abundance and prosperity in all its forms and should be done during a Waxing Moon. Keep the plant and crystal on a sunny ledge to draw prosperity, but scatter the anointed dimes, sharing the magic for others to find.

You will need:

- A green candle and candleholder
- A candle-carving tool
- Cinnamon or clove essential oil
- A potted basil plant
- 36 dimes
- A lighter or matches
- Candle snuffer
- An aventurine crystal
- A green ribbon

1. Cast your Circle (page 44). Cleanse, consecrate, and empower the candle, essential oil, plant, dimes, and crystal (page 32).

2. Carve the word "Prosperity" and your name on the candle and anoint it with the oil. Place the candle and the basil plant in front of you and surround them with a circle of dimes.

3. Light the candle and allow your breathing to become slower. Let your breath begin to open the realms of possibility within you. Believe you can attain prosperity. Know the Universe will open the door of abundance and that you are worthy to receive it in whatever form it may take.

4. When you are ready, hold the crystal in your power hand and begin this affirmation chant 36 times:

    I release all that does not serve me.

    The Goddess will fulfill my needs.

continued ▶

Prosperity Meditation Spell *continued*

Abundance and prosperity are all around me.

I radiate positive energy.

I am filled with hope.

I know that my future is bright.

I attract prosperity effortlessly.

I am healthy and filled with vitality.

I am open to all the wealth that is offered to me.

I am relaxed, calm, and at peace.

My life is filled with abundance.

I am grateful for all that I have received.

5. Put the crystal in the basil pot and tie the ribbon around the pot with 6 knots while saying an affirmation for each knot.

   Knot of one, my spell's begun.

   Knot of two, my dreams come true.

   Knot of three, abundance flows to me.

   Knot of four, I open prosperity's door.

   Knot of five, wealth will arrive.

   Knot of six, this spell is sealed and fixed!

6. When you are ready, snuff out the candle and release your Circle (page 46).

Early Spring Spell of Hope

This spell is intended to set your magickal intentions for the spring season and should be performed on the night of the New Moon.

You will need:

- 3 white candles and candleholders
- A candle-carving tool
- Rose geranium essential oil
- 3 small squares of parchment paper
- A felt-tip pen
- A lighter or matches
- Candle snuffer
- 3 large seeds
- 3 flowerpots
- 3 rose quartz crystals
- Potting soil
- 3 plant markers

1. Before you begin, take some time to think of three things you want to accomplish during the spring season.
2. Cast your Circle (page 44). Cleanse, consecrate, and empower the candles, seeds, and crystals (page 32).
3. Carve a Triskele into each white candle and anoint the candles with the essential oil. Draw a Triskele on each piece of paper.
4. Light the candles and chant three times three (9 times in total):

   Maiden Goddess of the spring

   New hopes and dreams you shall bring.

Triskele

continued ▶

Spells for the Solitary Wiccan 73

Early Spring Spell of Hope *continued*

5. Pick up one seed, hold it to your heart, and concentrate strongly on the intention that it represents. When you are ready, name the seed (e.g., happiness, knowledge), then write its purpose on one of the squares of parchment. Place the paper in the bottom of a flowerpot and put one crystal on top of it. Fill the pot with potting soil and plant the seed. Write the plant's name on a plant marker and place it in the flowerpot so you will remember which is which.

6. Continue in this manner with the other two seeds.

7. Place the three marked and planted pots in front of you and hold your hands over them while chanting three times three (9 times in total):

   As the Earth awakens and begins anew,

   Each seed a promise that will come true.

8. Snuff out the candles and release your Circle (page 46). Place the flowerpots in a sunny window and monitor their progress. As the seeds grow into plants, so shall your magickal intention grow. If one of the seeds doesn't sprout or fails to thrive, it may mean your purpose is not viable at this time.

Summer Spell of Courage

This spell will increase your personal courage and sovereignty throughout the summer season and is best done on a Tuesday (ruled by Mars) at noon, during a Waxing Moon.

You will need:

- A red candle and candleholder
- A candle-carving tool
- Dragon's blood essential oil
- A bloodstone crystal
- Dragon's blood incense
- 9 bulbs of garlic
- A lighter or matches
- Candle snuffer

1. Cast your Circle (page 44). Cleanse, consecrate, and empower the candle, crystal, and garlic (page 32).

2. Carve the Dragon Eye symbol on the candle and anoint it with the essential oil.

3. Place the candle, crystal, and incense in the center of your altar and surround them with the garlic. The combined energies of a red candle, dragon's blood incense and oil, Dragon Eye symbol, and garlic will generate a lot of courageous energy for you to tap into.

Dragon Eye

4. Light the candle and the incense. Breathe in the smell of dragon's blood—the scent of courage. Gaze into the flame of the candle—the color of courage. Pick up the bloodstone crystal—the stone of courage.

continued ▶

Summer Spell of Courage *continued*

5. Gaze into the candle flame and breathe deeply. Breathe in courage, breathe out fear and uncertainty. Visualize your body filling with the red fire of bravery with each inhalation and expelling fear with each exhalation. Continue until you feel filled with bravery, courage, and honor, with no anxiety remaining within you.

6. When you feel ready, repeat this chant three times three (nine times in total):

    Dragon's breath, and blood and smoke,

    A Dragon's courage I now invoke.

    Dragon's eye and candle red,

    Like skin of snake, the fear is shed.

    I am the dragon, I shall prevail,

    Bravery and valor will not fail.

    By my will, this spell is done,

    For the good of all, with harm to none!

7. Spend a few moments in meditation; perhaps you will receive a message from the Dragon. Listen with an open heart and mind.

8. When you are ready, snuff out the candle and release your Circle (page 46).

9. Bury the bulbs of garlic in a wild place so they may sprout and infuse the area with Dragon energy. If you can't plant them outdoors, place them in a flowerpot so you can harvest the bulbs when they mature and eat the magick of courage. Keep the bloodstone as a talisman of fearlessness. Rub it with dragon's blood essential oil periodically to recharge it.

Autumn Count Your Blessings Spell

This spell will affirm all the positive actions you have taken since Yuletide. Be sure to make the Gratitude Oil in advance.

You will need:

- Gratitude Oil (in a small glass vial, place ¼ ounce olive or grapeseed oil, 10 drops bergamot essential oil, 5 drops grapefruit essential oil, 5 drops cypress essential oil, 2 drops ylang-ylang essential oil, and 1 drop ginger essential oil, shake gently, and cap the vial)
- Large fallen leaves (one leaf for each gratitude)
- A red felt-tip pen
- A small paintbrush
- A gold ribbon

1. Make the Gratitude Oil several days before the Full Moon, then place it on a window ledge where it will receive both sunlight and moonlight.
2. On the night of the Full Moon, cast your Circle (page 44) and consecrate and empower the Gratitude Oil (page 32).
3. Spend some time considering all that you have learned and accomplished magickally and spiritually since Yule Sabbat.
4. Pick up all the leaves, hold them to your Heart Chakra, then raise them to the sky. Chant three times:

   Goddess and God, whom I adore,

   There is so much I'm thankful for.

   I've practiced my craft with harm to none

   For the highest good, my will was done.

   continued ▶

Autumn Count Your Blessings Spell *continued*

5. On each leaf, write one thing for which you are grateful. When you're finished, hold the bunch of leaves to your Heart Chakra and chant three times:

   Leaves that have fallen upon the ground,

   Now symbolize the thanks I have found.

6. With Gratitude Oil, paint an Earth-invoking Pentagram on each leaf to seal the charge.

7. Bundle the leaves together and tie the stems with the ribbon. Keep the leaves and Gratitude Oil on your altar to remind you of your accomplishments and to continue to show gratitude. Release your Circle (page 46).

8. To refresh the magick, add a few drops of oil to the leaves at every New and Full Moons. At Yule, take the bundle outdoors, burn it, and cast it into the winds.

Earth-invoking Pentagram

Winter Protection Spell: A Witch's Bottle

This spell will protect you, your home, and your sacred space throughout the dark winter months and should be done when the Moon is waning.

You will need:

- Dried marjoram, thyme, black pepper, mustard seed, yew
- Mortar and pestle
- A small glass bottle with a lid or stopper
- 9 onyx, hematite, or obsidian crystals (small enough to fit into the bottle)
- Tweezers
- Red thread cut into 3-inch lengths
- A few strands of your hair
- A small square of parchment
- A pen
- Patchouli essential oil
- Vinegar
- A black candle
- A lighter or matches
- Candle snuffer
- A Pentacle charm and black ribbon

1. Cast your Circle (page 44). Cleanse, consecrate, and empower the herbs, crystals, thread, hair, and essential oil (page 32).

2. While you are casting this spell, be sure to visualize protection and safety. Place the dried herbs into the mortar and begin crushing them with the pestle, being careful to move in a counterclockwise direction to banish. Chant nine times:

   Herbal protection starts to flow,

   Widdershins round the mortar go!

   continued ▶

Winter Protection Spell: A Witch's Bottle continued

3. Place the crushed herbs into the bottle.

4. One by one, add the crystals to the bottle and chant nine times:

    Protective stones as black as night,

    Baneful energy will take flight.

5. Using tweezers, add the red thread to the bottle and chant nine times:

    A tangled web of woven red,

    Protection set by strands of thread.

6. Using tweezers, add the strands of hair to the bottle and chant nine times:

    Hair of the witch, I put inside,

    Protection within shall now abide.

Eye Sigil   **Scythe Sigil**

7. On the parchment draw the sigils of Eye and Scythe and write your name and the date between them. Roll it up, add it to the bottle, and chant nine times:

    Eye of visions and scythe that rends,

    Defensive magick they shall lend.

8. Add nine drops of the essential oil to the bottle and chant nine times:

   Patchouli anchored to the ground,

   Magick spell cast and bound!

9. Add enough vinegar to fill the bottle one quarter of the way. Chant nine times:

   Vinegar sets the magick spell,

   Within this bottle, it shall dwell.

10. Cap the bottle, light the candle, and drip wax over the top of the bottle to seal it. Chant nine times:

    Defend, protect, preserve, and shield,

    Locked inside, the magick's sealed.

11. Tie the Pentacle charm onto the neck of the bottle, snuff out the candle, and release your Circle (page 46).

12. Place the bottle where you will see it and be reminded of its protective powers.

CHAPTER 5
WICCAN RITUALS FOR ONE

This chapter begins with a daily morning ritual that will instantly connect you with your inner Goddess and higher self. We'll explore the Turning of the Wheel through the observation of the Sabbats and the Moon Esbats. By performing these rites on their special days, you will join the collective energy created by Wiccans worldwide. You'll also learn about the Witch's Pyramid, connect with the Elements, and honor Mother Earth.

Morning Ritual

This ritual requires no tools or ingredients; its purpose is simply to begin each day by focusing on your Wiccan Path.

Focus on your breath for at least one minute. Count to five as you inhale, pause, and count to five as you exhale. Counted breathing creates balance and will bring your body into a state of deep relaxation.

1. When you are ready, give thanks to the Goddess and God. It can be as simple as saying: *I give thanks for the love of the Goddess and God.*

2. Turn to the East and say:

   Eastern Spirits of Air,

   You are the rising Sun of new beginnings,

   I am filled with inspiration and magick,

   I can communicate and concentrate,

   I am ready to begin today with confidence and joy!

3. Visualize yellow light shining from the East and filling your entire body. Spend a moment enjoying the Elemental energy of Air.

4. When you are ready, turn to the South and say:

   Southern Spirits of Fire,

   You are the blazing heat of the noonday Sun,

   I am filled with ambition and hope,

   I can transform and create,

   I am ready to begin today with purpose and authority.

5. Visualize red light shining from the South and filling your entire body. Spend a moment enjoying the Elemental energy of Fire.

6. When you are ready, turn to the West and say:

    Western Spirits of Water,

    You are the cooling waves of twilight,

    I am filled with love and acceptance,

    I understand and believe,

    I am ready to begin today with compassion and grace.

7. Visualize blue light shining from the West filling your entire body. Spend a moment enjoying the Elemental energy of Water.

8. When you are ready, turn to the North and say:

    Northern Spirits of Earth,

    You are the soothing black cloak of midnight,

    I am filled with well-being and patience,

    I am healed and balanced,

    I am ready to begin today with gentleness and peace.

9. Visualize green light shining from the North filling your entire body. Spend a moment enjoying the Elemental energy of Earth.

10. When you are ready, face the East once again, place your hands in a prayer position, and say:

    I give thanks for this day. Blessed be!

Samhain Sabbat Ritual

This solitary Samhain ritual marks the end of the Wiccan cycle and is a time to reflect on the past year's accomplishments and imperfections and release them so you may move forward.

You will need:

- A charcoal disc
- A lighter or matches
- Candle snuffer
- A cauldron or an incense burner
- A black candle, to represent the past
- A candle-carving tool
- An orange candle, to represent the future
- Peppermint essential oil
- 2 candleholders
- Dried mugwort

1. Cast your Circle (page 44). Light the charcoal disc and place it in the cauldron or incense burner.

2. Take the black candle and, beginning at the top, carve these words spiraling down to the bottom of the candle:

    I accept the past and all I've done, release, release, with harm to none.

3. Anoint the candle with the essential oil and place in a holder.

4. Take the orange candle and, beginning at the bottom, carve these words spiraling up to the top of the candle:

    I look ahead to the coming year, invoke, invoke, my future clear.

5. Anoint the candle with the peppermint essential oil and place in a holder.

6. Place the black candle to your left and the orange candle to your right.

7. Add the dried mugwort to the burning charcoal and invoke the Goddess:

   Crone Goddess at the edge of night,

   Descend to me and join my rite.

   You shelter me from my woes,

   You are the thorn, and you are the rose.

8. Take a moment to feel the change in energy now that the Crone has entered your Circle.

9. Light the black candle and gaze into it. Allow your eyes to go soft and unfocused as you reflect upon the past year. What lessons have you learned? In what ways have you grown? What could you have done better? When you are ready, snuff out the candle and bid farewell to the past year.

10. Light the orange candle, gaze into it, and visualize all that you wish to accomplish in the new year. When you are ready, snuff out the candle.

11. Thank the Goddess for joining you and release your Circle (page 46).

Yule Sabbat Ritual

This solitary ritual designed for the night of Yule marks the rebirth of the Sun and all the possibilities of new beginnings. It's a time for dreaming about what you will accomplish and planning for your Wiccan year.

You will need:

- 12 tea light candles arranged in a circle, to represent each month of the upcoming year
- A lighter or matches
- Candle snuffer
- A journal, grimoire, or Book of Shadows (optional)
- A pen (optional)

1. Cast your Circle (page 44).
2. Begin with the room in total darkness. Breathe in the stillness of the night and embrace the in-between time that occurs just before the dawning of a new day.
3. Say:

    It is the longest night of the year, yet tonight the Sun shall be reborn and carry me forward into the light of the new year. Apollo, Bel, Lugh, Balder, I call you into my Circle, may you bring illumination and joy!

4. Take a moment to feel the change in energy now that the Sun Gods have entered your Circle.
5. Light the first candle and say:

    I honor the month of January and the tide of renewal.

6. Light the second candle and say:

I honor the month of February and the tide of preparation.

7. Light the third candle and say:

    I honor the month of March and the tide of activation.

8. Light the fourth candle and say:

    I honor the month of April and the tide of awakening.

9. Light the fifth candle and say:

    I honor the month of May and the tide of growth.

10. Light the sixth candle and say:

    I honor the month of June and the tide of flowering.

11. Light the seventh candle and say:

    I honor the month of July and the tide of fulfillment.

12. Light the eighth candle and say:

    I honor the month of August and the tide of gratitude.

13. Light the ninth candle and say:

    I honor the month of September and the tide of harvest.

14. Light the tenth candle and say:

    I honor the month of October and the tide of recession.

15. Light the eleventh candle and say:

continued ▶

Yule Sabbat Ritual *continued*

I honor the month of November and the tide of remembrance.

16. Light the twelfth candle and say:

    I honor the month of December and the tide of consolidation.

17. When all the candles are burning, spend some time focusing on each month. Don't overthink it—allow impressions, visions, and thoughts to flow freely. If you wish, record your thoughts and ideas in your journal, grimoire, or Book of Shadows.

18. When you are ready, thank the Sun Gods for joining you, extinguish the candles, and release your Circle (page 46).

Imbolc Sabbat Ritual

This solitary Imbolc ritual marks the quickening of the Earth and the first whisper of spring. It's a great time to connect with the youthful Goddess and God as the Earth and all living things begin to respond to the lengthening days with anticipation and hope.

You will need:

- A white candle, to represent the Maiden Goddess
- A lighter or matches
- Candle snuffer
- 2 candleholders
- Fresh white flowers
- A green candle, to represent the Young God
- A small dish of honey
- Dried winter greenery
- A cauldron or heatproof container

1. Cast your Circle (page 44).
2. Light the white candle and invoke the Goddess:

   Maiden Goddess I call to thee,

   Honor my Circle,

   Please come to me.

   Innocent Maiden of purity and light,

   Honor my Circle

   With your presence tonight!

3. Place the flower offering in front of the Goddess candle.

continued ▶

Imbolc Sabbat Ritual *continued*

4. Light the green candle and invoke the God:

    Young God of the Greenwood, I call to thee,

    Honor my Circle,

    Please come to me.

    Young hero God, so brave and true,

    Honor my Circle

    As I honor you!

5. Place the honey offering in front of the God candle.

6. Take a moment to feel the change in energy now that the Goddess and God have entered your Circle.

7. Pick up the dried winter greenery and say:

    I say farewell to winter.

    May I share in the cycle of rebirth

    And blossom with new purpose and creativity.

8. Touch the greenery to the Goddess and God candles to light it on fire, then place it in the cauldron.

9. Once the greens have burned completely, say:

    So mote it be!

10. When you are ready, extinguish the candle, thank the Goddess and God for joining you, and release your Circle (page 46).

Ostara Sabbat Ritual

This solitary Ostara ritual marks the time when day and night are equal and balanced. The Wheel is turning toward the light, and the growing season will soon begin. It is a perfect time for you to show love, honor, and respect to the Earth Mother.

You will need:

- A pale green or pink candle
- A candleholder
- A pot of fresh spring flowers, such as crocus or daffodil
- A hard-boiled egg, colored and decorated any way you choose; the egg will be used as an offering, so keep your thoughts positive and happy while you're painting it
- A lighter or matches
- Candle snuffer

1. Cast your Circle (page 44).
2. Place the candle in front of you with the flowers to the left and the egg to the right.
3. Light the candle and say:

    Oh, Earth Mother,

    Source of all,

    Mother of all,

    You are fruit and flowers,

    Forests and rivers, oceans and rain.

    I am your child, anchored in your realm.

    Rejoice, for you are immortal and blessed with beauty,

continued ▶

Ostara Sabbat Ritual *continued*

Dressed in verdant green and crowned with stars.

Come, Earth Mother, and hear my prayer.

Draw near to me, O Goddess,

That I may receive your blessings on this night of balance.

4. Take a moment to feel the energetic change now that the Goddess has entered your Circle.

5. Hold the decorated egg in both hands. Visualize white light beaming down from above and entering your body through your Crown Chakra. Continue until you feel filled with light.

6. Begin to transfer the light into the egg with your will; it may begin to feel warm, your hands may start to tingle, or you may feel nothing at all. You may see it glow or pulse with light, or it may sparkle and vibrate. Whatever you see or feel, believe in your heart that you have enchanted the egg with positive energy and it is a worthy offering to the Earth Mother.

7. When you are ready, nestle the egg in the flowerpot.

8. The remainder of this ritual will be outdoors, but before you can continue, you must extinguish the candle and release your Circle (page 46).

9. Take the egg and flowerpot outdoors to leave as an offering to the Earth Mother. As you place the offering, say:

Please accept this enchanted offering, filled with magick and my love for you. Blessed be, beautiful Mother!

Beltane Sabbat Ritual

This solitary Beltane ritual is a celebration of the sacred union of the Goddess and God, of love, fertility, and fire. Beltane marks the beginning of the light half of the year, and this ritual will help you spread light and joy to the world.

You will need:

- A white taper candle
- A candle-carving tool
- Rose or rose geranium essential oil
- A candleholder
- 8 pastel-colored ribbons, 12 to 16 inches long (or 5 inches longer than the candle)
- A red felt-tip pen
- A glass-head straight pin or thumbtack
- 8 fresh roses
- 8 strawberries
- 8 rose quartz crystals

1. Cast your Circle (page 44).

2. Beginning at the bottom of the candle, carve the following words in a spiral up to the top of the candle:

    - Love, love, love
    - Your name
    - The date
    - Beltane Sabbat
    - Love, love, love

3. Anoint the candle with the essential oil and place it in the holder.

continued ▶

Beltane Sabbat Ritual *continued*

4. Think of eight things you could do to share love, joy, and happiness over the next year. It could mean visiting an elderly relative, doing random acts of kindness, giving an anonymous gift to someone, or volunteering—whatever is feasible for you.

5. Write each action on a separate ribbon.

6. Hold the completed ribbons to your Heart Chakra and chant eight times:

Eight for the Sabbats, ribbons, and rhymes,

My intentions are pure.

From my heart, the light shines,

It shall grow and endure.

Beltane is a night filled with love,

Goddess and God bless this work that I do,

By Earth, Moon, and stars that twinkle above.

My heart's filled with hope, and my motives are true.

One ribbon per Sabbat is the magick I've sown,

The spell starts at Litha, and goes till Beltane,

When the ribbons are gone, the spell will be done,

The spell will increase, the magick remains.

Throughout the seasons the energy grows,

Eight is the charm that sets the spell fast,

With harm to none, I do will it so!

Eight is the end and eight is the last!

7. Fasten the ribbons to the top of the candle with the pin so it resembles a maypole, then encircle it with the roses, strawberries, and crystals.

8. Spend a few moments enjoying the energy you have created. When you are ready, release your Circle (page 46).

9. You will not light the Maypole candle until next year at Beltane, when the spell is complete. At each Sabbat, remove a ribbon and carry out your act of love as you've promised, then tie the ribbon to a tree branch and leave it there, along with one of the crystals.

Litha Midsummer Sabbat Ritual

This solitary Litha ritual is a celebration of the Sun God at the height of his power and should be performed outdoors at noon.

You will need:

- 2 clear quartz crystals
- A gold-colored pouch or bag

1. Cast your Circle (page 44).

2. Facing South with arms outstretched and a crystal in each hand, allow the energy of the Sun to embrace you. Feel the warmth of the Sun on your skin. Begin a rhythm of slow, deep breathing as you consciously relax your body. Continue breathing deeply until you feel calm, centered, and totally present in the moment.

3. When you are ready, visualize golden light beaming down from the Sun and entering your body through your Crown Chakra. Feel the strength and power of the Sun God as the light enters your body. Visualize the light expanding out and enveloping you in a sphere. When you can clearly see the field of light energy around you, begin to turn your body sunwise (clockwise) three times while chanting:

I honor the God of the Sun,

My body is filled with His light.

4. When you stop circling, face South. Hold the crystals up to the Sun until you can feel that they are filled with the Sun's power. Hold the stones to your Heart Chakra and recite this prayer:

Lord of the Sun, whose loving embrace of the Earth Mother

Heats Her earthen womb to bring forth the bounty of fruits and flowers,

As you flame within the summer sky, you are within my heart and soul.

May you bring me the warmth of your love,

All the days of my life.

May you illuminate that which is shrouded in darkness

And burn away all that no longer serves me.

I dedicate these crystals to you, God of Light,

That they shall be my physical reminder of this day,

As the Wheel shall turn, at the season's progress.

So mote it be!

5. When you are ready, thank the Sun God, then release your Circle (page 46). Place the crystals in the pouch as your personal talismans of Sun God energy. You can recharge the stones periodically throughout the year by placing them in sunlight.

Lammas Sabbat Ritual

This solitary Lammas ritual celebrates the first harvest and the combined powers of the Goddess and God with the ceremony of bread and wine.

You will need:

- 1 gold candle, to represent the God
- 1 green candle, to represent the Goddess
- Frankincense essential oil
- 2 candleholders
- A chalice or cup filled with red wine or grape juice
- A small loaf of bread or a corn muffin
- Athame
- A lighter or matches
- Candle snuffer

1. Anoint the candles with the essential oil and place them in the holders. Put the gold candle, athame, and bread on the right and the green candle and chalice on the left.

2. Cast your Circle (page 44).

3. Light the Goddess candle and say:

   Goddess of the Harvest,

   Earth Mother, I honor you.

   Please join me in my rite.

4. Light the God candle and say:

   God of the Harvest,

   Sun God, I honor you.

   Please join me in my rite.

5. Take a moment to feel the change in energy now that the Goddess and God have entered your Circle.

6. When you are ready, hold the athame in your right hand and say:

    Essence of the God blessed be!

7. Hold the chalice in your left hand and say:

    Essence of the Goddess blessed be!

8. Plunge your athame into the chalice and say:

    This wine has been blessed by Their sacred union.

9. Take a sip of the wine and say:

    Through this wine, I receive Their blessings.

10. Pick up the loaf of bread and say:

    Essence of the Goddess and God blessed be!

11. Eat a piece of the bread and say:

    Through this bread, I receive Their blessings.

12. Spend a few moments in meditation and give thanks for all that you have received.

13. When you are ready, thank the Goddess and God for their presence, extinguish the candles, and release your Circle (page 46).

Mabon Sabbat Ritual

This solitary Mabon ritual is one of perfect balance; day and night are equal at this moment in time. As you prepare for the winter ahead, it is an excellent time to give thanks and show gratitude. A thankful heart will bring light and peace into your life.

You will need:

- 1 gold candle
- A dish of salted water
- A candle-carving tool
- A candleholder
- A lighter or matches
- Candle snuffer
- A black felt-tip pen
- Dried leaves large enough to write on

1. Cast your Circle (page 44).

2. Anoint the candle with the salted water and say:

    Goddess of Water and Earth

    Shall cleanse and purify

    The God of Fire and Air.

3. Beginning at the bottom of the candle and spiraling up to the wick, carve your name, the date, and the words *Thank you for blessings received*.

4. Place the candle in the holder, light it, and say:

    Tonight, I pause to give thanks for all that I have been given.

    I invite the Goddess and the God into my Circle of thanksgiving.

5. Take a moment to feel the change in energy now that the Goddess and God have entered your Circle.

6. When you are ready, spend a few moments in meditation thinking about everything you're grateful for in your life. Write it all down on the dried leaves.

7. Hold the leaves to your Heart Chakra and chant three times three (nine times):

   Mabon balances the day and the night,

   We welcome the darkness and release the light.

   I have counted my blessings; I'm grateful for all,

   As summer light fades to the chilled air of fall.

   I give you my honor, my trust, and my love;

   As below, it shall be as it is above!

8. Extinguish the candle and release your Circle (page 46). Continue the rest of this rite outdoors.

9. Take the dried leaves outside and find a private spot where you won't be disturbed.

10. Facing North, hold the leaves up to the sky and turn slowly clockwise three times while chanting:

    Into the Northern spirit winds,

    I release these blessings given to me.

    As Autumn begins and summertime ends,

    I am ready for winter; my spirit is free!

11. Release the leaves into the wind and walk away without looking back.

The Witch's Pyramid Ritual

The Witch's Pyramid is a philosophy of magick and a spiritual way of being. It is: To Know, To Will, To Dare, and To Keep Silent. This ritual can be done during any Moon phase and is intended to illuminate ways in which you have already been practicing the Witch's Pyramid without really knowing or understanding it.

You will need:

- A journal or Book of Shadows
- A pen

1. Cast your Circle (page 44) and sit comfortably in the center. Begin breathing deeply and rhythmically until you feel calm, centered, and relaxed. Focus on the following steps and actions.

2. **To Know:** This is the first step of the pyramid. It is a clear intention. It can also be thought of as your Wiccan knowledge and your commitment to seek wisdom and truth throughout your life. Knowing can also mean psychic awareness through dreams, your subconscious, and psychic visions.

3. In your journal, write down 10 essential things about Wicca that you know.

4. **To Will:** This is the second step of the pyramid. It is the focus of your thoughts and the visualization of what you want and how you will get it. It can also be thought of as the way that you make use of the collective energy available to you through the correspondences of crystals, herbs, oils, the Elements, and deity. It is also the will to carry on in the face of adversity and obstruction.

5. In your journal, write down 10 things that were obstacles in the way of your chosen Wiccan Path and how you overcame them.

6. **To Dare:** This is the third step of the pyramid. It is the process of doing the magick. It can also be thought of as daring to be Wiccan. It took courage for you to seek out Wicca and begin walking your spiritual path. You also dare to call the Gods into your sacred space, raise power for spells, and explore your motives and emotions.

7. In your journal, write down 10 things about Wicca that required the most courage for you to do.

8. **To Keep Silent:** This is the fourth step of the pyramid. It is the power of listening and saying nothing, heeding the inner voice of wisdom, and allowing the magick of your spell to work without speaking about it to others. There is a belief that if you talk about your spell, you will call it back to you before its magick is completed.

9. In your journal, write down 10 instances when you did not remain silent, and the consequences, if any, that you experienced.

10. Spend some time in reflection upon the lessons of the Witch's Pyramid. Listen with an open heart to any messages, thoughts, or ideas you receive.

11. When you are ready, release the Circle (page 46).

Elemental Ritual

This ritual is intended to bring you to a deeper understanding of the Elements of Earth, Air, Fire, and Water, and it can be done during any Moon phase.

You will need:

- 1 stick of incense of your choice
- An incense holder
- A lighter or matches
- Candle snuffer
- 1 feather
- 1 red votive, pillar, or taper candle
- 1 candleholder
- 1 seashell
- 1 stone or crystal of your choice
- A journal
- A pen

1. Cast your Circle (page 44) and sit comfortably in the center.

2. Light the incense. Begin to breathe deeply and rhythmically. Let your breath calm your inner voices, soothe your spirit, and release your thoughts and worries. Continue deep breathing until you feel calm, centered, and relaxed.

3. Spend a few moments thinking about Air. It is associated with the early light of dawn, the season of spring, and the East. The Element of Air is masculine and represents thoughts, ideas, and conceptions. It is the base of the Witch's Pyramid, **To Know.** Air is all around you, moving in and out of your body with each breath you take, yet it is often invisible. Wave the feather near the incense, and you will see the air move the smoke.

4. Light the candle, place it in the holder, and spend a few moments thinking about Fire. The Element of Fire is masculine and is associated with the burning heat of noon, the season of summer, and the South. It is the second step of the Witch's Pyramid, **To Will.** You can feel its power on your skin when you stand in the heat of the Sun. Stretch out your fingers to the flame and feel the essence of fire.

5. Pick up the shell and spend a few moments thinking about Water. It is associated with twilight, the season of autumn, and the West. The Element of Water is feminine and represents healing, emotion, and reaction. It is the third step of the Witch's Pyramid, **To Dare.** Water is the lifeblood of all living things, without which we could not live. It is cleansing, healing, and nurturing. Place the shell to your ear and hear the sound of the eternal sea.

6. Pick up the stone and spend a few moments thinking about Earth. It is associated with the velvet cloak of midnight, the season of winter, and the North. The Element of Earth is feminine and represents integration, wisdom, growth, prosperity, and understanding. It is the fourth step of the Witch's Pyramid, **To Keep Silent.** The Earth is our Mother, who provides us with shelter and nourishment. If you like, stretch out your tongue and taste the essence of Earth Mother.

7. Spend a few moments in meditation while you experience the presence of the Elements within your Circle.

8. When you're ready, write your impressions, ideas, and thoughts in your journal. Extinguish the candle and release the Circle (page 46).

Solitary Full Moon Esbat Ritual

This ritual will connect you with the power of the Full Moon through the sacred act of creating Moon Water, which is used to purify and cleanse sacred space, tools, and supplies. Moon Water is traditionally placed on the ritual altar to represent the Element of Water and the West. If you like, make a new batch of Moon Water each month, but don't discard the old; instead, treat it with respect and add a little to the new batch, pour it into your ritual bathwater, or give it to the Earth as an offering to Gaia.

You will need:

- A silver or white candle
- A lighter or matches
- Candle snuffer
- A candleholder
- A crystal or glass bowl
- A pitcher or container of clear water
- Natural sea salt

1. Cast your Circle (page 44) and spend a few moments considering the Full Moon, allowing the power and lunar energy presence to saturate your mind, spirit, and emotions.

2. Light the candle, place it in the holder, and invite the Goddess into your Circle:

   I call the Mother Goddess,

   Queen of Heaven and of Earth,

   Mother of all wisdom and magick,

   Whose love flows down upon me

   Carried upon the rays of the Moon.

   Blessed be the Goddess!

3. Take a moment to feel the change in energy now that the Goddess has entered your Circle. Sit silently for a few moments and commune with Her.

4. Fill your crystal bowl with the water and add a pinch of salt. Charge the water with your intent by holding your hands over it while visualizing the mixture filling with positive, loving Moon Goddess energy. See the water overflow with Her Spirit. Take your time and really see this happen.

5. When you're ready, thank the Moon and the Goddess, kiss your fingers, and hold them up to the Moon three times—one for the Maiden, one for the Mother, and one for the Crone. Snuff out the candle and release your Circle (page 46).

6. Take your newly charged Moon Water outside to an unobstructed moonlit area and leave it there overnight. If you can't leave the bowl outdoors, place it near a window that receives moonlight. In the morning, bottle your newly made Moon Water and store it in a dark place.

The River of Love Ritual

This ritual will create a river of love from you to the Earth and its many forms and beings. Perform this ceremony on the night of the Full Moon or when the Moon is waxing.

You will need:

- A pink candle
- Rose essential oil
- 1 stick of lavender or rose incense
- An incense burner
- A lighter or matches
- Candle snuffer
- A candleholder

1. Cast your Circle (page 44), anoint the candle with the essential oil and place it in the holder, then light the candle and incense.

2. Sit quietly for a moment and breathe deeply, in through your nose and out through your mouth. Consciously release all thoughts and emotions. Surrender to the beauty and wisdom of this moment, knowing you are safe and protected within your Magick Circle.

3. Say:

   I am a strong and powerful Wiccan. I know that I have the power and the right to send and receive love. May the Goddess and God help and bless this work that I shall do, may it harm none and be for the good of all.

4. Feel the loving energy that is streaming into you from the Goddess and God. Breathe in that love and let the joy and light fill you. Their love for you is the spark of creation from which we were

born, and the light of this love is what connects us, one to another, and to Them, through all time.

5. Imagine sharing the love-light that fills you. Visualize a river of love flowing freely from your Heart Chakra to the Earth and all who live upon it. There is an endless supply of this energy, and you will always have more than you need. Sustain this visualization for as long as you can.

6. When you are ready, allow the energy flow to slow and then stop. Know in your heart and soul that your offering of love has been received and accepted.

7. Extinguish the candle and release your Circle (page 46).

Plant Familiar Ritual

This ritual will help you create a plant familiar that will be able to retrieve energies, information, and messages for you from the herbal realm. Choose your seeds wisely; if you want your plant to live longer than a year, select a perennial rather than an annual. Pick seeds that resonate with you magickally and spiritually.

You will need:

- A flowerpot with drainage tray
- Potting soil
- A small glass of water
- A small quartz crystal or stone
- Seeds of your choosing, depending upon your goal:
    - Angelica: perennial; for protection, healing, psychic visions
    - Basil: annual; for love, wealth, banishing
    - Chamomile: perennial; for calm, sleep, purification
    - Geranium: annual; for fertility, health, love
    - Lavender: perennial; for purification, peace, happiness, protection
    - Marigold: annual: for prophesy and psychic powers
    - Peppermint: perennial; for purification, love, healing, supernatural powers
    - Snapdragon: annual; for protection
    - Thistle: perennial; for strength, exorcism, banishing, healing

1. Half an hour before you begin this ritual, fill the flowerpot with loosely packed potting soil and place it in the drainage tray. Pour warm water into the tray so the soil will become evenly moist. Put the glass of water on a windowsill where it will receive full sun so the energy of the God may bless it.
2. Gather all ingredients and cast your Circle (page 44).

3. With the water glass held in your power hand, lift it into the sunlight and say:

   God of the Sun shall bless the Water.

   Blood of the Goddess, blessed by the Sun,

   Sun of the God alive in the water,

   The Goddess and God now are one!

4. With the crystal in your power hand, hold it in the sunlight and say:

   God of the Sun shall bless the crystal.

   Body of the Goddess, blessed by the Sun,

   Sun of the God alive in the body,

   The Goddess and God now are one!

5. Plant some of the seeds in the pot, following the instructions on the packet.

6. Pour some of the Sun-blessed water on the freshly planted seeds. Gently tap the pot three times and say:

   By the combined powers of the Goddess and God

   Shall these seeds awaken and grow

   To become my Plant Familiar!

continued ▶

Plant Familiar Ritual *continued*

7. Place the crystal in the plant pot and say:

   Earth and Fire combined as one,

   Strengthen the seeds when growth's begun.

   Protect and encourage this brand-new life,

   Bud and stem and root and leaf.

8. Gently blow on the plant pot three times and say:

   Earth, Fire, Water, and Air.

   All the Elements this plant will share.

   This spell is fixed, this spell is done,

   With blessings, love, and harm to none!

9. When you are ready, release your Circle (page 46).

10. Place the pot on a sunny windowsill or in the greenhouse if you have one. Nurture it carefully, and soon you will have your very own Plant Familiar.

New Moon Ritual of Artemis

Perform this ritual on the night of the New Moon to petition the Goddess Artemis for spiritual guidance.

You will need:

- 1 white flower (such as a rose) in a water-filled vase
- A silver chalice of water (if possible, draw the water from a moving river or stream)
- 1 stick of incense of your choice
- An incense holder
- 2 silver or white candles
- 2 candleholders
- A lighter or matches
- Candle snuffer
- 1 moonstone or selenite crystal

1. Cast your Circle (page 44).
2. Place the vase with the flower, chalice, and incense in the center of your altar with the candles on either side.
3. Breathe deeply for a few moments to ground and center yourself. Light the candles and the incense.
4. Invoke the presence of Artemis by reciting this prayer six times (six is Her sacred number):

   I call to Artemis, whose arrows are shafts of gold

   And whose bow is the Crescent Moon,

   Pure and virginal maiden, wild and free,

   Artemis, huntress who follows the stag,

   In the lone places by rivers and streams,

   continued ▶

New Moon Ritual of Artemis *continued*

With your hounds gifted to you by the Great God Pan.

Come, Maiden Goddess, I invite you into my Circle.

5. Take a moment to feel the change in energy now that Artemis has entered your Circle.

6. When you are ready, dip the crystal into the chalice, touch your forehead, and say:

    Artemis, Goddess of the New Moon,

    Help me understand the soul of Nature and honor it during this Moon Cycle.

7. Dip the crystal into the chalice, touch each of your eyelids, and say:

    Artemis, Goddess of the New Moon,

    Help me see the path to follow this Moon Cycle that I may grow in my craft.

8. Dip the crystal into the chalice of water, touch your heart, and say:

    Artemis, Goddess of the New Moon,

    Help me listen to my heart that I may grow in my craft.

9. Dip the crystal into the chalice, touch the palms of each of your hands, and say:

    Artemis, Goddess of the New Moon,

    Help my hands work your magick that I may grow in my craft.

10. Dip the crystal into the chalice, touch the tops of your feet, and say:

   Artemis, Goddess of the New Moon,

   Help me travel your hidden paths with love and light, that I may grow in my craft.

11. Hold the crystal to your Heart Chakra and say:

    I dedicate this crystal to the Goddess Artemis.

    It shall be a tool of New Moon magick.

12. When you are ready, thank Artemis for her presence, extinguish the candles, and release your Circle (page 46).

13. Place the vase with the flower on your bedside table as a reminder of your visit with the Goddess. Keep the crystal as a personal New Moon talisman.

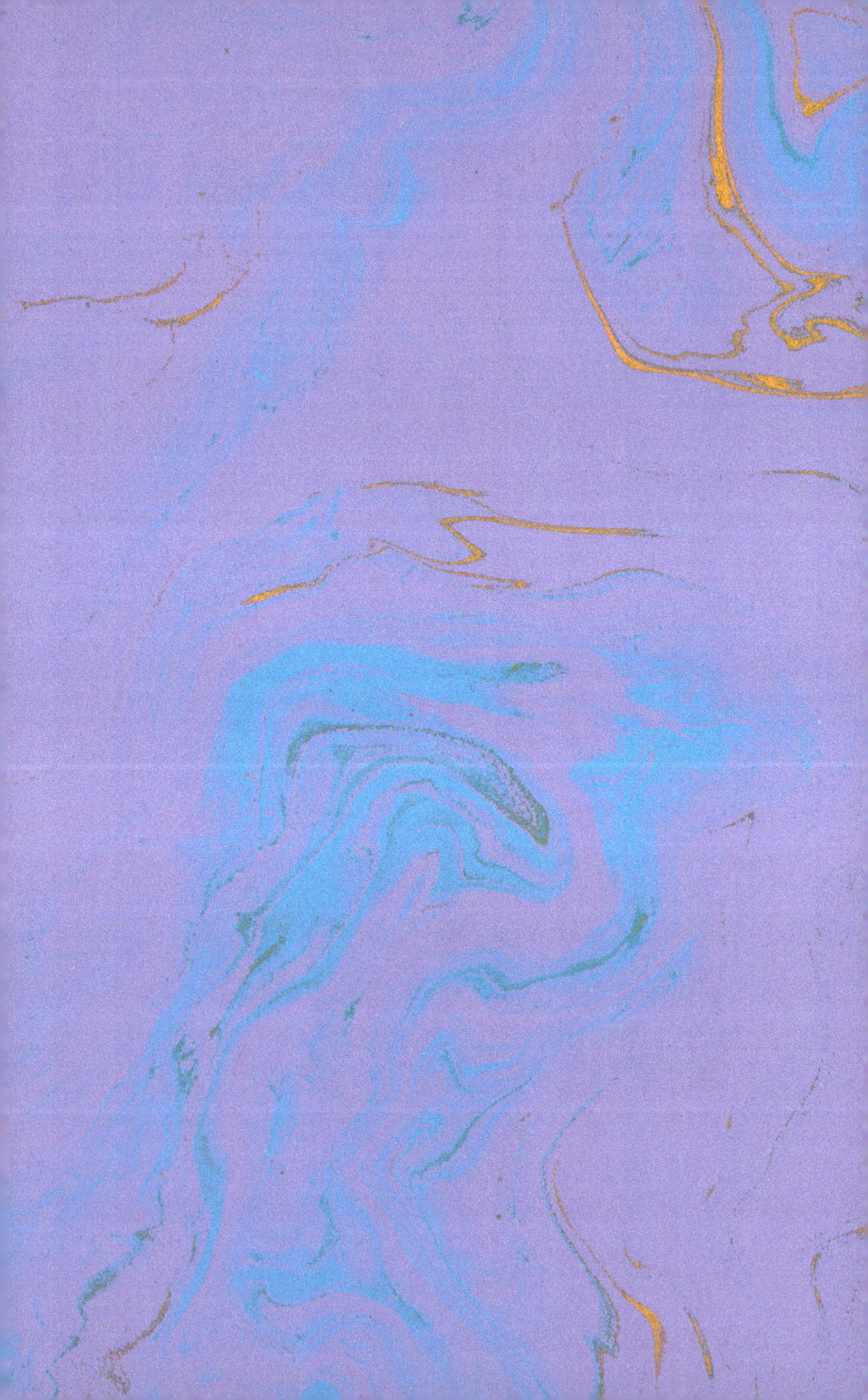

CHAPTER 6
RECIPES FROM THE SOLITARY KITCHEN

This chapter explores the joy of combining the magick spice of your intention and food. Mindful cooking will not only nourish your body but will also feed your spiritual connection to the God and Goddess and to your Wiccan practice. Gathering ingredients, understanding their inherent metaphysical properties, and transforming them through the alchemy of cooking is a simple way for you to pass the magick on to those who eat the enchanted food. In turn, they will carry the magick with them out into the world.

Samhain Soul Cakes

Makes 6 cakes / Prep time: 10 minutes / Cook time: 25 minutes

At Samhain, Wiccans traditionally honor ancestors and the spirits of loved ones who have passed. Soul cakes are round spice cakes with an X in the center known as the equal armed cross, a mark made to remember the dead. You can eat them during your Sabbat Ritual, use them as offerings on your altar, or leave them outdoors for wandering spirits to eat. You can also set an extra place at your table with a plate of Soul Cakes for your lost loved ones so you may enjoy a meal together.

- ½ cup (1 stick) unsalted butter, softened
- ½ cup granulated sugar
- 2 egg yolks
- 1¼ cups all-purpose flour, plus more for dusting
- 1 teaspoon allspice
- ½ teaspoon pumpkin pie spice
- 2 tablespoons whole or evaporated milk
- ¼ cup black or red currants or chopped raisins

Before you begin, take a few moments to honor ancestors and spirits with this simple prayer:

> *On Samhain night, I will remember*
>
> *My ancestors, my loved ones, and all the witches*
>
> *Who have passed through the veil.*
>
> *May they feel welcome and loved.*
>
> *In the names of the Goddess and God*
>
> *I will make these Soul Cakes as an offering to them,*

That they shall receive sustenance

And know that they are not forgotten.

So mote it be!

1. Preheat the oven to 350°F. Coat a baking sheet with nonstick cooking spray and set aside.
2. Cream the butter and sugar until light and fluffy.
3. Fold in the egg yolks, flour, allspice, and pumpkin pie spice until evenly combined.
4. Add the milk a little at a time, stirring until the dough holds together.
5. Gently mix in the raisins or currants.
6. On a lightly floured surface, roll the dough out to a ½-inch thickness.
7. Cut out the cakes with a round cookie or biscuit cutter and transfer to the prepared baking sheet.
8. Using a knife, mark each cake with an equal-armed cross. Cut the first line directly down the center of the cake and say:

   This represents the line between the living and the dead

   Carve the second line and say:

   This line represents the intersection of life and death on Samhain night. So mote it be!

9. Bake for 25 minutes, or until golden and firm.

Recipes from the Solitary Kitchen

Yule Gingerbread Magick Charm Cookies

Makes 36 cookies / Prep time: 10 minutes, plus 2 hours to chill / Cook time: 15 minutes

At Yule, there is no better way to honor the spirit of the Sabbat than by sharing these spiced cookies. Ginger has the magickal properties of healing, love, passion, success, prosperity, and protection; the cloves and nutmeg uphold ginger's protection and health benefits; and the cinnamon boosts the magickal power of the herbs.

You can cut the cookies into a variety of shapes and decorate them with icing, sprinkles, or candies. Once they are baked, you can pipe runes, sacred symbols, words, or pictures to indicate their magickal purpose. To enchant your cookies with your goal, remember to visualize your intention throughout the process. Enchanted cookies make a wonderful gift.

For the Cookies

- 1 teaspoon ground ginger
- ½ teaspoon ground cloves
- ¼ teaspoon nutmeg
- 1 teaspoon cinnamon
- ½ cup brown sugar
- ¾ cup molasses
- ½ teaspoon salt
- ¾ cup (1½ sticks) unsalted butter
- 1 beaten egg
- 3⅓ cups flour, plus more for dusting
- 1 teaspoon baking soda

For the Icing

- 1½ cups powdered sugar
- 1 teaspoon vanilla extract
- 1 teaspoon light corn syrup
- 2 to 2½ tablespoons room temperature water
- Pinch of salt

1. Preheat the oven to 350°F. Coat a baking sheet with nonstick cooking spray and set aside.
2. In a large double boiler, combine the ginger, cloves, nutmeg, cinnamon, brown sugar, molasses, and salt.
3. Cook over medium heat, stirring constantly, until the mixture comes to a boil. Be sure to stir only in a clockwise direction; this draws positive energy, while stirring counterclockwise banishes negative energy.
4. Remove from the heat. Mix in the butter.
5. Add the egg and mix well.
6. Fold in the flour and baking soda until well mixed.
7. Transfer the dough to a bowl, cover, and chill in the refrigerator for at least 2 hours.
8. On a lightly floured surface, roll out the dough to a ¼-inch thickness.
9. Use a cookie cutter to cut out shapes. Transfer to the prepared baking sheet.
10. Bake for 12 to 15 minutes. Let cool.
11. Make the cookie icing, if desired. Blend the powdered sugar, vanilla, corn syrup, and 2 tablespoons water in a medium bowl. It should be thick, but add a bit more water if it is not spreadable. If it is too thin, add a bit more powdered sugar.
12. Spread on the cookies or transfer to a piping bag and decorate as desired.

The Magickal Shapes

Call upon these magickal shapes and associations in your baking to infuse your creations with even more potent power.

Animal—sacrifice

Bell—protection, spirit world

Bird—peace, messenger

Circle—unity, infinity, protection

Crescent Moon—The Goddess, clairvoyance

Cross—balance, life

Flower—tranquility

Heart—love

Oval—fertility, growth, expansion

Rectangle—stability, grounding, Earth magick, growth

Spiral—spirituality

Square—foundation, grounding, the Elements, equality

Star—protection, truth, knowledge, banishing, healing, cleansing, psychic power

Sun—The God, growth

Triangle—Triple Goddess, manifestation, power, binding

Brigid's Imbolc Custard

Makes 4 (6-ounce) custards / Prep time: 10 minutes / Cook time: 40–55 minutes

Imbolc Sabbat is a celebration associated with the Goddess Brigid and the beginning of spring. The word Imbolc is from the Old Irish *oimelc*, meaning ewe's milk. February was typically the time when the lambing season would begin and fresh milk would again become available.

This simple and delicious custard incorporates pagan symbolism with a surprise coin hidden in one of the custards. Be sure to eat carefully! Whoever gets the custard cup with the coin will receive extra blessings, but with blessings come obligations. You must toss the coin into a well or a natural body of water to complete the magick.

- One nickel (sanitized in boiling water and cooled)
- 2 cups milk, room temperature
- 2 eggs, room temperature
- ¼ cup granulated sugar
- ¼ teaspoon vanilla extract
- Pinch salt
- ¼ teaspoon nutmeg
- ¼ teaspoon cinnamon

1. Preheat oven to 325°F. Consider your oven as a representation of Brigit's sacred hearth fire. As it is heating, recite this prayer:

    I will build the hearth

    As Brigid would build it.

    Guarding the hearth, guarding the floor,

    Guarding the household all!

2. Place four 6-ounce custard cups in a baking pan that is at least 2 inches deep.

continued ▶

Brigid's Imbolc Custard *continued*

3. Put the nickel in the bottom of one cup.

4. Heat the milk to scalding, but not boiling, in a saucepan on the stove or in the microwave.

5. Using a wire whisk, stir together the milk, eggs, sugar, vanilla, and salt.

6. Divide the mixture evenly among the baking cups.

7. Fill the baking pan with hot water even with the top of the custard. The pan of water can be thought of as the Wiccan magickal cauldron of transformation. To honor this concept, hold your hands over the pan and visualize the fires of Brigit's hearth combining with the cauldron's waters to heat and transform the custard from liquid to solid.

8. Mix the nutmeg and cinnamon in a small bowl. Sprinkle on top of the custard.

9. Bake for 40 to 55 minutes, or until the custard is set. Test the custard by inserting a knife into the center, which should come out clean.

10. When you turn off the oven, say this final prayer to honor Brigit and your oven hearth:

I will smore the hearth

To save, to shield, to surround,

The hearth, and the household,

Tonight, and every night.

Blessed be!

Ostara Magick Eggs

Makes 6 eggs / Prep time: 30 minutes

Ostara marks the day when day and night are equal and balanced. The Maiden Goddess celebrates her youth and freedom as the sun's strength increases. The egg is a symbol of fertility, balance, promise, new life, and rebirth, so it's the perfect food to use as an offering and an edible spell. The enchanted eggs may be eaten, gifted, placed on your altar, or left outdoors as a gift to the Earth Mother.

- 6 hard-boiled eggs
- Food coloring or natural egg dye
- Magic markers, paints, or stickers
- Small basket to hold the finished eggs

1. Before you begin, decide what you want your eggs to represent magickally, such as healing, love, and prosperity.
2. Dye and decorate each egg in turn, being sure to visualize your intention throughout the entire process.
3. Place basket of eggs on the altar. Pick up your athame and say:

   In the names of the Goddess Ostara,

   And the Lord of the Greenwood,

   By the power of the Four Elements

   Air, Fire and Water and Earth,

   I bless these eggs!

4. Point your athame at each egg and make a sign of the Earth-invoking Pentagram: Visualize energy flowing from you through the blade of your athame into each egg.

Earth-invoking Pentagram

Natural Egg Dyes and Magickal Colors

Use this helpful guide to dye your eggs with natural materials and learn what each color brings to your magickal working.

Blue represents wisdom, healing, truth, protection, dream magick. Create natural dyes using crushed blueberries or water in which red cabbage has been boiled.

Light blue represents peace, tranquility, spiritualism.

Green represents fertility, Earth magick, prosperity. Create natural dyes using water in which spinach has been boiled.

Lavender represents blessings, divination, peace, protection, wisdom. Create natural dyes using grape juice or violet blossoms mixed with a small amount of lemon juice.

Orange represents abundance, beginnings, confidence, courage, success, justice, strength. Create natural dyes using water in which yellow onion skins, paprika, or chili powder have been boiled.

Pink represents friendship, love, peace, fidelity.

Red represents ambition, courage, strength, lust, love, rebirth, willpower, Goddess energy. Create natural dyes using pomegranate or raspberry juice.

Yellow represents action, change, communication, happiness, optimism, purification, God energy. Create natural dyes using water in which lemon peels, carrot tops, ground cumin, or turmeric have been boiled. You can also use chamomile or green tea.

Recipes for Beltane Sabbat

Beltane Sabbat is all about love. It's a day for fertility rites, lighthearted celebration, love-chases, maypole dancing, and honoring the sacred union of the Goddess and God.

Lavender Sugar

Makes 1 cup / Prep time: 5 minutes, plus 1 week to rest

A pinch of lavender sugar adds magick to any food. Lavender's powers include love, protection, sleep, purification, joy, and peace.

- 1 cup granulated sugar
- 2 to 5 tablespoons fresh or dried lavender buds

1. Pour the sugar into a small bowl.
2. Crush the lavender buds between your hands to release the flavor and scent.
3. Use a spoon to fold the crushed buds into the sugar.
4. Transfer to a jar and seal tightly.
5. For full flavor, allow to rest at least a week before using.

Strawberry Jam Love Spell

Makes 6 (1-pint) jars / Prep time: 15 minutes / Cook time: 1 hour

Strawberries, vanilla, lemon, and sugar are the perfect magickal foods to invoke love, along with a suitable spell.

- 2 pounds fresh large strawberries, hulled
- 4 cups granulated sugar
- 1 tablespoon vanilla extract
- ¼ cup lemon juice

1. In a large bowl, using a fork or potato masher, crush the berries into a rough pulp. Use a fork to draw a heart shape in the pulp and say:

   Red strawberries filled with desire,

   Passion's flames will stoke the fire,

   Love, sweet love will come to me

   With harm to none, so mote it be!

2. Combine strawberries, sugar, vanilla, and lemon juice in a medium saucepan. Simmer the jam mixture over low heat, stirring constantly, until the sugar is evenly dissolved and the jam has a smoother consistency.

3. Increase the heat to medium and bring to a full boil.

4. Boil, stirring often, about 45 minutes, until the jam reaches 220°F (105°C).

5. Transfer to hot, sterile jars and seal tightly.

Eat the jam right away or store in the refrigerator for up to 1 month.

Cupid's Carrot Cake

Makes 1 (9-inch) cake / Prep time: 25 minutes / Cook time: 45 minutes

Promoting fertility and lust, carrot cake is the perfect Beltane fare.

- 1 cup all-purpose flour
- 1 teaspoon baking soda
- ¼ teaspoon fine sea salt
- ¾ teaspoon ground cinnamon
- 1 cup plus 2 tablespoons vegetable oil
- ½ cup granulated sugar
- ½ cup brown sugar
- ½ teaspoon vanilla extract
- 2 large eggs
- 1½ cups peeled and grated carrots
- ½ cup coarsely chopped pecans or walnuts
- ¼ cup raisins

1. Preheat the oven to 350°F. Grease and flour a 9-inch cake pan.
2. In a medium bowl, combine the flour, baking soda, salt, and cinnamon.
3. In a separate bowl, combine the oil, granulated sugar, brown sugar, and vanilla.
4. Add the eggs to the sugar mixture one at a time, beating until evenly combined.
5. Add the dry ingredients in 3 parts, stirring at each interval, until the dry ingredients are well incorporated and the batter is smooth.
6. Gently fold in the carrots, pecans or walnuts, and raisins.
7. Pour the batter into the prepared pan. Bake for 35 to 45 minutes or until a toothpick inserted into the center comes out clean.

Litha Fire Cider Tonic

Makes 1 quart / Prep time: 30 minutes

At Litha, or Summer Solstice, the bright summer sunlight is the living symbol of the Sun God. You can capture the sun's magick for later use by creating a batch of Fire Cider tonic on Solstice Day. It will be ready by Mabon and will fortify your body with the Sun God's energy throughout the dark half of the year. Drink 1 tablespoon of tonic every day to ingest the power of the summer Sun.

God Ingredients:

- ½ cup freshly grated organic ginger root, for power and success (Fire Element)
- ½ cup freshly grated organic horseradish root, for purification (Fire Element)
- 1 medium organic onion, chopped, for healing (Fire Element)
- 10 organic garlic cloves, crushed or chopped, for protection and healing (Fire Element)
- 1 fresh whole oak leaf, for healing (Fire Element)
- ¼ teaspoon organic cayenne powder, for protection (Fire Element)
- 2 tablespoons dried rosemary leaves, for healing (Fire Element)
- 2 organic jalapeño peppers, chopped, for protection (Fire Element)

Goddess Ingredients:

- Zest and juice from 1 organic lemon, for purification (Water Element)
- 1 tablespoon organic turmeric powder, for purification (Water Element)
- Pinch of mugwort, for healing (Earth Element)
- Pinch of vervain, for cleansing (Earth Element)

Other Ingredients:

- Organic apple cider vinegar
- ¼ cup raw honey, or to taste

1. Place the roots, fruits, whole oak leaf, and herbs in a quart-size glass jar.
2. Pour the vinegar in the jar until everything is covered and the vinegar reaches the top.
3. Use parchment paper under the lid to keep the vinegar from touching the metal.
4. Shake well.
5. To charge your finished tonic with Sun God energy:

    Hold the tonic up to the Sun and chant three times three (9 times)

    Apollo, Sol, Helios,

    I draw down the Sun

    Into this vessel.

    May your power flow within it.

    Blessed be!

6. Store in a refrigerator until Mabon Sabbat.
7. Shake your tonic daily.
8. At Mabon, use cheesecloth to strain out the pulp, squeezing out as much liquid as possible.
9. Transfer the tonic to a clean jar.
10. Add honey to taste, if desired.

Lammas Bread Magick

Makes 2 (5-by-9-inch) loaves / Prep time: 20 minutes, plus rising / Cook time: 35 minutes

Lammas is the celebration of the grain harvest and the magickal alchemy of baking bread through the application of the four Elements. Earth is the mixture of flour and salt; Air is the yeast. When Water is added, the mixture becomes a liquid, and the alchemy of Fire changes it back into a solid.

- 4½ teaspoons active dry yeast
- ¼ cup warm water
- ½ cup honey
- 3 teaspoons salt
- 2½ cups hot water
- ¼ cup (½ stick) unsalted butter
- 4½ cups whole wheat flour, divided
- 2¾ cups all-purpose flour, plus more for dusting

1. In a small bowl, dissolve the yeast in the warm water, stirring clockwise.
2. In a large bowl, combine the honey, salt, hot water, and butter. Let cool slightly, then add 3 cups whole wheat flour.
3. Mix until just combined, then beat for 3 minutes at medium speed.
4. Add the remaining 1½ cups whole wheat flour and dissolved yeast, and mix thoroughly, until flour is evenly combined
5. Stir in 2¼ to 2¾ cups all-purpose flour until the dough pulls cleanly away from the bowl.
6. On a floured surface, knead in ½ to 1 cup all-purpose flour until the mixture is smooth and elastic.
7. Place the dough in a greased bowl. Cover with plastic wrap and a clean kitchen towel.

8. Let rise in a warm place until doubled in size (30 to 45 minutes).
9. Grease 2 loaf pans.
10. Punch down the dough to remove air bubbles.
11. Divide the dough into two equal parts and shape into loaves.
12. Place in pans, cover with a clean towel, and let rise in a warm place until doubled in size (30 to 45 minutes).
13. Preheat the oven to 375°F.
14. Bake for 30 minutes, reduce the oven to 350°F, and bake for an additional 10 to 15 minutes. The loaves are done when they sound hollow when lightly tapped.
15. Remove from the pans and cool on a wire rack.
16. Enchant the loaves by holding your hands above them and chanting three times:

Air into Water, with reverence and mirth

Water and Air is blended with Earth,

Transformed into bread by alchemy's Fire,

The Elemental alliance will achieve my desire.

Bread is the body of the God upon Earth,

From the womb of the Mother, the grain's given birth,

The promise fulfilled from Spring's early dawn,

The spirit of life through the grain shall live on!

Mabon Sabbat Recipes

Mabon Sabbat is a celebration of the second harvest and thanksgiving, but it is also tinged with sadness. The God has begun his slow descent into the Underworld, and the grieving Goddess withdraws fertility from the Earth. With its properties of abundance, bounty, wisdom, and guidance, the apple embodies both the thanksgiving energies of Mabon and, with its associations with the Underworld and rebirth, the sorrowful aspects of this Sabbat as well.

Mabon Apple Cake

Makes 1 (9-by-13-inch) cake / Prep time: 15 minutes / Cook time: 50 minutes

The apple is sacred to Mabon Sabbat as a symbol of the fruit harvest and signifies immortality, healing, and rebirth. Cut an apple horizontally and you will discover the secret Pentagram hidden within.

- 2 large eggs, room temperature
- 1 cup granulated sugar
- ¾ cup brown sugar
- 2 teaspoons cinnamon
- ½ teaspoon ginger
- Pinch of ground cloves
- 1 teaspoon vanilla
- ½ teaspoon salt
- ½ cup vegetable oil
- 6 medium apples
- 2 cups all-purpose flour
- 2 teaspoons of baking soda

1. Preheat the oven to 350°F. Grease a 9-by-13-inch pan and set aside.
2. In a large bowl, mix the eggs, granulated sugar, brown sugar, cinnamon, ginger, cloves, vanilla, salt, and oil.

3. Peel and core, the apples, then slice into eighths. To prevent browning, add them to the cake mixture as you go.

4. Add the flour and mix gently with a fork until all the flour is absorbed.

5. Transfer the batter to the prepared pan. Using a knife, draw an Earth-invoking Pentagram on top of the batter and say this prayer:

Earth-invoking Pentagram

This cake represents my love for the Goddess and God.

As their strength begins to wane and the Earth turns away from the Sun,

May this food of the Gods sustain me in my Wiccan faith

During the coming winter months, that I may witness

The Goddess transformed and the God reborn.

So mote it be!

6. Bake for 50 minutes or until a toothpick or knife inserted into the cake comes out clean.

Mabon Wishes Applesauce

Makes 6 cups / Prep time: 10 minutes / Cook time: 20 minutes

Mabon is a time for making jams, jellies, and sauces from the bounty of the fruit harvest. In some traditions, there's a belief that your fate for the next twelve months is sealed on Mabon night. To ensure that your future is bright, cook up this applesauce recipe with a secret ingredient—a fresh sage leaf to make your wishes come true.

- 4 apples, peeled, cored, and sliced into eighths
- ¾ cup water
- ¼ cup granulated sugar
- 1 to 2 teaspoons cinnamon
- 1 fresh sage leaf

1. Place the apples, water, sugar, and cinnamon in a saucepan.
2. To empower the sage leaf:
    - Hold it to your heart and visualize your wish as completed.
    - Continue with this visualization for as long as you can.
    - Trust that the sage leaf has absorbed your wish and will enchant your applesauce with your desire.
3. Add the sage leaf, cover the saucepan, and cook over medium heat until the apples are soft.
4. Allow apples to cool, then remove sage leaf and mash the softened apples with a fork or potato masher.
5. Eat and share the applesauce to complete the spell.

Drinkable Magick: Tea for Every Intention

You can make magick with a cup of tea: Simply infuse the herbs in boiling water, empower the brew, and drink the spell. Here you'll find teas for a range of desires and needs.

For each of your teas, use the following method:

1. Place the herbs in a teapot and add boiling water.
2. Steep for 10 to 15 minutes.
3. Strain the herbs and pour the tea into a cup.

Attract Love Tea

- 1 teaspoon dried red rose petals or 3 teaspoons fresh
- ½ teaspoon dried jasmine flowers or 1½ teaspoons fresh
- ½ teaspoon dried raspberry leaves or 1 teaspoon fresh

Empower the tea by stirring and chanting several times:

Goddess Aphrodite, I ask of thee

Grant me love

As I drink this tea!

Banishing Tea

- 1 teaspoon dried cloves
- 1 single peppercorn
- 1 teaspoon dried nettle or 3 teaspoons fresh

Empower the tea by stirring and chanting several times:

Goddess Hecate, I ask of thee

Banish negative energies

As I drink this tea!

Courage Tea

- 1 teaspoon dried borage or 3 teaspoons fresh
- 1 teaspoon dried thyme or 3 teaspoons fresh

Empower the tea by stirring and chanting several times:

Goddess Athena, I ask of thee

Grant courage and strength

As I drink this tea!

Divination Tea

- 3 teaspoons orange peel
- 3 teaspoons pomegranate seeds

Empower the tea by stirring and chanting several times:

Goddess Hecate, I ask of thee

Grant me clairvoyance

As I drink this tea!

Healing Tea

- 1 teaspoon dried lemon balm or 3 teaspoons fresh
- 1 dried bay leaf or 3 fresh

Empower the tea by stirring and chanting several times:

Goddess Brigit, I ask of thee

Grant healing and health

As I drink this tea!

Happiness Tea

- 1 teaspoon dried catnip or 3 teaspoons fresh
- 1 teaspoon dried lavender or 3 teaspoons fresh

Empower the tea by stirring and chanting several times:

Goddess Hathor, I ask of thee

Grant happiness and joy

As I drink this tea!

Lucky Tea

- ½ teaspoon nutmeg spice
- 1 teaspoon orange peel
- 1 whole star anise

Empower the tea by stirring and chanting several times:

Goddess Fortuna, I ask of thee

Grant me good luck

As I drink this tea!

Prosperity Tea

- ½ teaspoon dried rosemary or 1½ teaspoons fresh
- ½ teaspoon dried basil or 1½ teaspoons fresh
- ½ teaspoon dried peppermint or 1½ teaspoons fresh
- ½ teaspoon dried blackberry leaves or 1½ teaspoon fresh

Empower the tea by stirring and chanting several times:

Goddess Abundantia, I ask of thee

Grant prosperity

As I drink this tea.

Protection Tea

- 1 teaspoon dried angelica leaves or 3 teaspoons fresh
- 1 dried bay leaf
- 5 whole cloves
- 1 teaspoon dried fennel seeds

Empower the tea by stirring and chanting several times:

Mother Goddess I ask of thee

Grant protection

As I drink this tea!

Honey Rose Elixir

Makes: 1 pint / Prep time: 30 minutes, plus 4 weeks to rest

Create a delicious honey rose elixir to use in your altar chalice when you are creating love and healing magick. Take a teaspoonful at a time during your rituals to help ease a broken heart, soothe anxiety, or cope with grief.

- 1-pint mason jar with lid
- Rose petals
- ⅔ cup honey
- 1 pint vodka

1. Gather enough rose petals during a Full Moon to fill a pint jar.
2. Add honey to the jar and stir.
3. Top up the jar with the vodka.
4. Cap the jar and shake several times to mix.
5. Hold the jar up to the moonlight and chant nine times:

    I dedicate this elixir to the Goddess of love,

    The Goddess of beauty, and roses, and doves,

    I honor Aphrodite on this Full Moon night,

    May this potion become an enchanting delight!

6. Place the elixir in a cool, dark place until the next Full Moon.
7. Strain, bottle, and label your Honey Rose Elixir.

Lavender Lemonade

Makes 2 cups / Prep time: 15 minutes, plus 2 hours to chill

This potion, which should be made on the night of a Full Moon, is a spell of attraction that uses lemon for love and drawing helpful spirits; lavender for love, happiness, and peace; and sugar for even more love and lust.

- ½ cup dried lavender
- 2 cups boiling water
- Juice of 2 lemons
- ½ cup granulated sugar

1. Place the lavender in a pitcher and add the boiling water.
2. Stir clockwise nine times while chanting:

   Lavender flowers of scented delight,

   Lend me your magick on this Full Moon night.

3. Cover the pitcher and place it where it will receive direct moonlight.
4. Let steep for 15 minutes, then discard the lavender flowers.
5. Add the lemon juice and sugar and stir until the sugar is dissolved.
6. Refrigerate at least 2 hours, until chilled through.

Chocolate Mousse Happiness Spell

Makes 4 (½-cup) servings / Prep time: 20 minutes, plus 1 hour to chill

Dark chocolate combines the Elemental energies of Earth and Fire and the magickal properties of love, romance, grounding, and prosperity. This delicious dark chocolate confection is just the trick to banish unhappiness.

Light a pink candle, place it near where you'll cook, and put on some joyful music. You may want to dance around for a few minutes, allowing your body to release tension and draw in positive energy through movement and sound. Before you begin, consider why you are feeling unhappy. On a small square of paper, write down those reasons, then fold the paper and hold it to your heart as you say this prayer:

> *I ask that the Goddess and God*
>
> *Enfold me in their love and acceptance.*
>
> *Please help me lift this veil of sorrow,*
>
> *And embrace the joyfulness inherent in life!*
>
> *As I will it, it is so!*

- 1 pound dark chocolate, finely chopped
- Zest of 1 orange
- 2 tablespoons orange liqueur (such as triple sec or Grand Marnier)
- 2 eggs, well beaten
- 2 cups whipping cream, whipped

1. In a double broiler, stir the chocolate until it has completely melted.
2. Coat the folded paper with the melted chocolate, then set aside. The chocolate coating has sealed in the negativity written on the paper.
3. Add the orange zest, orange liqueur, and eggs, and stir until smooth.
4. Gently fold in the whipped cream.
5. Divide evenly among ramekins or glasses.
6. Chill for at least 1 hour before serving.

While you are waiting for your dessert to set, take the chocolate covered paper outdoors, if possible, and bury it. If you can't go outside, flush it down the toilet.

Candied Flowers

Prep time: 30 minutes, plus 24 hours to dry

Candied flowers are a versatile, edible tool for offering to the Gods, adding to food or drink, or attaching to candles to help boost intention.

- Edible flowers or petals of your choice (see Flower Magick, page 149)
- 1 egg white
- 1 teaspoon water
- Fine sugar

1. Gather the flowers during the appropriate Moon phase:
   - New Moon: Maiden Goddess, new beginnings, new opportunities
   - Waxing Moon: growth, success, abundance, healing, love, money
   - Full Moon: Mother Goddess, fullest potential for all magick, healing, protection, intuition, dreams, ancestors, Deity invocation, water magick
   - Waning Moon: banishing, decreasing, diminishing, releasing, cleansing
   - Dark Moon: Crone Goddess, fullest potential of banishing

2. Rinse the flowers and let dry on a clean cloth.

3. Put the egg white and water in a small bowl and whisk together. Put a few teaspoons of sugar in a separate bowl. Once the flowers are fully dry, dip each one in the egg wash, then roll in sugar to coat evenly.

4. Place the flowers on wax paper and allow to dry for 24 hours.

5. Store in an airtight container in single layers with wax paper between each layer.

Flower Magick

Read on to discover which flower will serve your magickal purpose.

Bergamot petals: money, wealth, success

Borage flowers: courage, psychic powers, family and home, peace and tranquility

Calendula petals: love potions, protection, consecration, psychic powers

Chamomile (German) flowers: sleep, money, anti-hexing, purification, protection

Chicory petals: removing obstacles, invisibility, thrift, prophetic dreams

Chive flowers: intuition, psychic powers, love, well-being

Clover flowers: protection, money, love, fidelity, exorcism, success

Cornflower petals: psychic powers, third-eye awakening, self-knowledge, spirituality

Dandelion petals: divination, wishes, calling spirits

Dianthus petals: protection, strength, healing

Hibiscus petals: lust, love, divination

Hollyhock petals: growth, fertility, rebirth, wealth

Johnny Jump Up (*Viola tricolor*) flowers: protection, luck, love, lust, wishes, peace, healing

Lavender flowers: happiness, love, blessings, divination, peace, wisdom, protection

Lilac flowers: exorcism, protection

Nasturtium petals: aspiration, strong beliefs, ethics, festivity

Pansy flowers (*Viola* x *wittrockiana*): ease a broken heart, love, cheerfulness

Pea flowers (the edible garden variety, not sweet peas): friendship, protection (especially of children)

Phlox perennial flowers (*Phlox paniculata*): family harmony, courage, productivity

Primrose (*Primula vulgaris*): faerie sightings and spells, beauty, charisma, rejuvenation

Rose petals: beauty, love, affection, divination, healing, magick

Squash flowers: creativity, vitality, healing, balance

Sunflower petals: luck, truth, loyalty, honesty, fertility, faeries

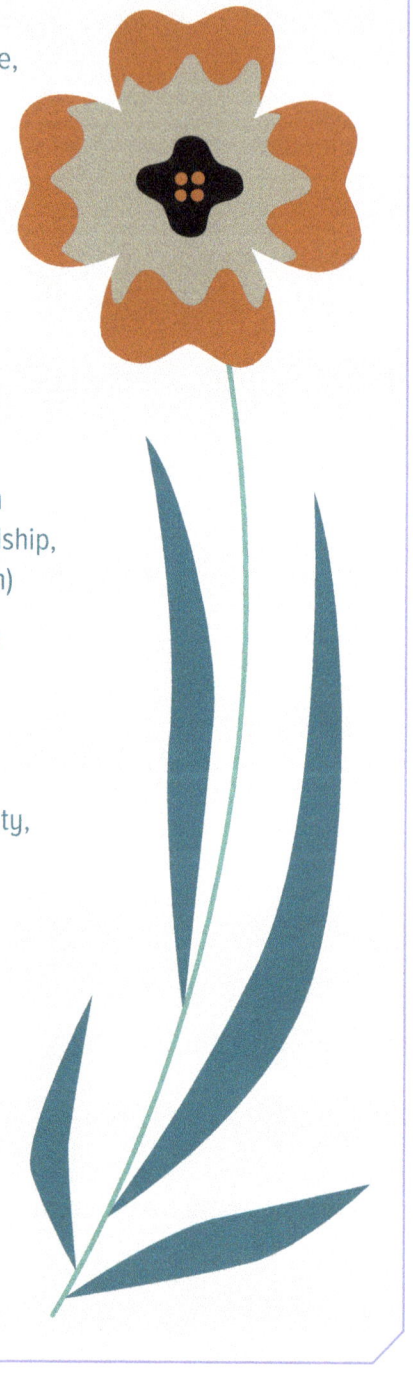

Banishing Potion Spell

This drinkable spell will help you banish negative thoughts and energies. Cast it when the Moon is waning to take advantage of the Moon tides of decrease.

- A chalice or glass
- Juice from 3 lemons
- Pinch of dried peppermint
- Pinch of dried rosemary
- Wooden spoon

1. To set your intention, softly chant three times:

    I make this vow upon this night,

    Baneful energy will take flight

    When I drink this potion down

    Cares and woes sink to the ground.

2. Squeeze the lemons and pour the juice into the chalice.

3. Add the peppermint and rosemary and stir counterclockwise (the direction of banishing) while chanting:

    Peppermint shall purify

    And rosemary shall exorcise

    Bound within the lemon pure

    Baneful energy will not endure.

4. Your magick potion is now ready to be consumed.

Simple Syrups for Magick

Simple syrups are another delicious way to internalize potent magickal energy. Be sure to infuse it with your intention (see below) during the cooking process and to bless it before you eat it. Magick syrup can be drizzled over cakes, pancakes, and ice cream or added to club soda, lemonade, iced tea, hot tea, or plain water.

- 1 cup granulated sugar
- 1 cup water
- 12 ounce bottle
- 1½ cups fresh or frozen fruit of your choice, peeled, washed, and cut into small pieces

1. Bring the sugar, water, and prepared fruit to a boil.
2. Reduce the heat and simmer for 25 minutes or until the fruit is softened and breaking down.
3. Stir occasionally with a wooden spoon in a clockwise direction while meditating on the energetic properties you want to instill into your syrup.
4. Remove from heat and pour the mixture through a fine-mesh strainer.
5. Let cool completely.
6. Bottle and store in the refrigerator for up to 1 month.

Fruit Magick

While all fruit is glorious, each carries its own magickal uses for your workings.

Apple: love, healing, fidelity, immortality, garden spells

Blackberry: healing, wealth, protection, sex

Blueberry: acceptance, home blessings, luck, peace

Cherry: clarity, creativity, divination, psychic energy, romance

Fig: protection, luck, sleep, fertility

Grape: dreams, fertility, intellect, spiritual energy, wealth

Grapefruit: cleansing, confidence, healing, courage, purification

Kiwi: happiness, health, longevity, love, romance

Lemon: longevity, purification, love, friendship, psychic powers

Mango: balance, harmony, marriage, romance

Nectarine: love

Orange: beauty, divination, luck, money

Peaches: innocent love, pleasure, wealth, well-being

Pear: abundance, wealth, thanksgiving

Plum: love, protection, anti-negativity, relaxation

Raspberry: protection, love, relationships, courage, dreams

Strawberry: love, luck, happiness, success

Greenman Wild Nettle Soup

Serves 4 / Prep time: 30 minutes / Cook time: 35 minutes

Align your energies to the spirit of the Greenman by making nettle soup. Nettle is a fantastic spring tonic and magickal herb of protection with a potent sting (so be careful!). When harvesting nettles, be sure to wear long sleeves and thick gloves, and pick only the young, tender leaves and shoots. The leaves will lose their sting after you boil them for five minutes.

- 1 tablespoon olive oil
- 1 onion, finely chopped
- 1 pound potatoes, peeled and diced
- 8 ounces nettle leaves
- Salt
- Freshly ground pepper
- 6 cups chicken broth
- Nutmeg, for serving

1. Heat the oil in a large soup pot over medium heat until shimmering. Reduce the heat to low and sauté the onion and potatoes gently until soft but not browned.
2. Add the nettle leaves and salt and pepper to taste.
3. Cover and cook for 5 minutes.
4. Add the chicken broth and bring mixture to a boil.
5. Simmer for 30 minutes, or until potatoes and onion are cooked through.
6. Process with an emulsifier blender or pour into a food processor and blend until smooth.
7. Sprinkle with nutmeg before serving.

CHAPTER 7
THE SOLITARY WICCAN APOTHECARY

In this chapter you'll learn how to prepare oils, incense, salves, powders, charm bags, and more! Don't forget to share: you can give away your apothecary items to family and friends as favors and charms.

Wiccan Oils

Create your own sacred Sabbat oils to anoint yourself, candles, tools, spell crafting items, and sacred objects such as tarot cards, jewelry, talismans, or amulets. Dab or paint magickal symbols on documents, book pages, and spell papers, or add a few drops to your ritual bathwater.

The following oil recipes are specially blended to align with the ritual energy of each Sabbat.

For each oil recipe, you will need:

Eyedropper

5 ml glass bottle with lid

Essential oils (specific to each recipe)

Base oil of your choice:

- **Almond:** prosperity, money, wisdom (Air Element)
- **Avocado:** love, emotions (Water Element)
- **Coconut:** purification, protection (Water Element)
- **Grape seed:** fertility, wealth, intellect (Water Element)
- **Hemp seed:** healing, love, psychic, meditation (Water Element)
- **Jojoba:** healing, love (Water Element)
- **Olive:** healing, peace, fertility, protection (Fire Element)
- **Sunflower:** protection, fertility, health, wisdom (Fire Element)

Samhain Sabbat Oil

A special blend to assist communication between you and your loved ones while providing protection and comfort. As you mix the oils, visualize the sacred spirit of Samhain.

You will need:

- 4 drops pine oil
- 7 drops lavender oil
- 3 drops frankincense oil
- 1 drop patchouli oil
- 1 onyx or obsidian crystal
- Base oil of your choice (page 158)

1. Using an eyedropper, put the pine, lavender, frankincense, and patchouli oils in the bottle.
2. Add the crystal.
3. Fill the bottle with the base oil.
4. Cap the bottle, label, and store in a cool, dry place.

Yule Sabbat Oil

Embrace the season of long winter nights while invoking the warming spirit of hearth, home, fire, and spirit. As you mix the oils, visualize the sacred spirit of Yule.

You will need:

- 6 drops frankincense oil
- 3 drops cedarwood oil
- 2 drops orange oil
- 4 drops clove oil
- 1 pine, fir, or cedar needle
- Base oil of your choice (page 158)

1. Using an eyedropper, put the frankincense, cedarwood, orange, and clove oils in the bottle.
2. Add the needle.
3. Fill the bottle with the base oil.
4. Cap the bottle, label, and store in a cool, dry place.

Imbolc Sabbat Oil

A blend to ignite the flames of creativity as the Earth's energy begins to shift from the cold darkness of winter toward sunlight and spring. As you mix the oils, visualize the sacred spirit of Imbolc.

You will need:

- 5 drops jasmine oil
- 7 drops rose oil
- 3 drops lemon oil
- 1 chamomile flower
- 1 jasmine flower
- Base oil of your choice (page 158)

1. Using an eyedropper, put the jasmine, rose, and lemon oils in the bottle.
2. Add the flowers.
3. Fill the bottle with the base oil.
4. Cap the bottle, label, and store in a cool, dry place.

Ostara Sabbat Oil

This blend evokes vitality, inspiration, and new beginnings. It will inspire your soul as the Earth's energies shift into spring. As you mix the oils, visualize the sacred spirit of Ostara.

You will need:

- 8 drops orange oil
- 5 drops vanilla oil
- 2 drops ylang-ylang oil
- 1 small amethyst crystal
- Base oil of your choice (page 158)

1. Using an eyedropper, put the orange, vanilla, and ylang-ylang oils in the bottle.
2. Add the crystal.
3. Fill the bottle with the base oil.
4. Cap the bottle, label, and store in a cool, dry place.

Beltane Sabbat Oil

A blend that will ignite the fires of creativity, passion, and love as you dance, sing, and make merry during this joyful season. As you mix the oils, visualize the sacred spirit of Beltane.

You will need:

- 3 drops lemon oil
- 3 drops jasmine oil
- 2 drops lavender oil
- 3 drops lemongrass oil
- 3 drops rose geranium oil
- 3 drops ylang-ylang oil
- 1 small rose quartz crystal
- Base oil of your choice (page 158)

1. Using an eyedropper, put the lemon, jasmine, lavender, lemongrass, rose geranium, and ylang-ylang oils in the bottle.
2. Add the crystal.
3. Fill the bottle with the base oil.
4. Cap the bottle, label, and store in a cool, dry place.

Litha Sabbat Oil

Invoke the long, lazy days of summer and the spirit of the Lord and Lady of the Greenwood. This sacred blend will promote luck and prosperity during this season of growth and abundance. As you mix the oils, visualize the sacred spirit of Litha.

You will need:

- 5 drops lavender oil
- 4 drops chamomile oil
- 3 drops rose geranium oil
- 3 drops sandalwood oil
- 1 chamomile flower
- Base oil of your choice (page 158)

1. Using an eyedropper, put the lavender, chamomile, rose geranium, and sandalwood oils in the bottle.
2. Add the flower.
3. Fill the bottle with the base oil.
4. Cap the bottle, label, and store in a cool, dry place.

Lammas Sabbat Oil

An uplifting and cleansing blend to honor the season of heat, light, and warmth. As you mix the oils, visualize the sacred spirit of Lammas.

You will need:

- 4 drops lime oil
- 4 drops rose geranium oil
- 3 drops lavender oil
- 2 drops sandalwood oil
- 2 drops dragon's blood oil
- 1 small citrine crystal
- Base oil of your choice (page 158)

1. Using an eyedropper, put the lime, rose geranium, lavender, sandalwood, and dragon's blood oils in the bottle.
2. Add the crystal.
3. Fill the bottle with the base oil.
4. Cap the bottle, label, and store in a cool, dry place.

Mabon Sabbat Oil

As the Earth prepares for her long winter's slumber, honor the shifting energy of the season with this oil. Visualize the sacred spirit of Mabon as you mix the oils.

You will need:

- 9 drops frankincense oil
- 4 drops orange oil
- 2 drops cinnamon oil
- 1 apple seed
- Base oil of your choice (page 158)

1. Using an eyedropper, put the frankincense, orange, and cinnamon oils in the bottle.
2. Add the apple seed.
3. Fill the bottle with the base oil.
4. Cap the bottle, label, and store in a cool, dry place.

Wiccan Salves

To further empower your work, make your own special salves using the magick of flowers and herbs. Once you've tried out the following recipes, begin to concoct your own salves by choosing specific herbs and essential oils that resonate with you. To use the salves, rub on pulse points, feet, or back of the neck.

Wiccan Dream Salve

As you make this salve, know that each herb has been chosen to ease your path into the meditative state and pierce the veil of dreams.

You will need:

- ⅓ ounce dried mugwort
- ⅓ ounce dried yarrow
- ⅓ ounce dried wormwood
- 1 cup extra virgin olive oil
- A 16-ounce mason jar
- A strainer
- Cheesecloth
- 1 ounce beeswax, shaved into thin strips
- A glass measuring cup
- 5 drops jasmine essential oil (optional)
- 10 drops sandalwood essential oil (optional)
- A small jar or tin

1. Heat the herbs and olive oil over very low heat in a double boiler or slow cooker for 1 to 3 hours.
2. Strain the herbs by pouring the mixture into the mason jar through a strainer lined with cheesecloth, squeezing to recover all the oil.

continued ▶

Wiccan Dream Salve *continued*

3. Discard the herbs or tie them up in the cheesecloth to use as a bath sachet.

4. Melt the beeswax in a double boiler over low heat, being careful not to let it burn.

5. Pour the melted wax into the infused olive oil and mix well.

6. Transfer the mixture to the measuring cup.

7. Add the essential oils, if using.

8. Pour into the small jar and label.

9. Store the salve in a cool, dark place for up to 9 months.

Rosebud Love Salve

Roses are sacred to Aphrodite and Venus, the Goddesses of love. As you create this uplifting, sexy salve be sure to empower it with love, love, love.

You will need:

- 1 ounce dried red rosebuds
- 1 cup extra virgin olive oil
- A 16-ounce mason jar
- A strainer
- Cheesecloth
- 1 ounce beeswax, shaved into thin strips
- A glass measuring cup
- 15 drops rose or rose geranium essential oil (optional)
- 1 drop patchouli essential oil (optional)
- A small jar or tin

1. Heat the rosebuds and olive oil over very low heat in a double boiler or slow cooker for 1 to 3 hours.
2. Strain the rosebuds by pouring the mixture into the mason jar through a strainer lined with cheesecloth; be sure to squeeze the rosebuds to recover all the oil.
3. Discard the rosebuds or tie them up in the cheesecloth to use as a bath sachet.
4. Melt the beeswax in a double boiler over low heat, being careful not to let it burn.
5. Pour the melted wax into the infused olive oil and mix well.
6. Transfer the mixture to the measuring cup.
7. Add the essential oils, if using.
8. Pour into the small jar and label.
9. Store the salve in a cool, dark place for up to 9 months.

Protection Salve

This salve's herbs have been chosen for their protective, banishing, and healing properties.

You will need:

- ⅓ ounce dried nettle leaves
- ⅓ ounce dried carnation petals
- ⅓ ounce dried peony petals
- 1 cup extra virgin olive oil
- A 16-ounce mason jar
- A strainer
- Cheesecloth
- 1 ounce beeswax, shaved into thin strips
- A glass measuring cup
- 8 drops lavender essential oil (optional)
- 8 drops orange essential oil (optional)
- A small jar or tin

1. Heat the herbs and olive oil over very low heat in a double boiler or slow cooker for 1 to 3 hours.
2. Strain the herbs by pouring the mixture into the mason jar through a strainer lined with cheesecloth, squeezing the herbs to recover all the oil.
3. Discard the herbs or tie them up in the cheesecloth to use as a bath sachet.
4. Melt the beeswax in a double boiler over low heat, being careful not to let it burn.
5. Pour the melted wax into the infused olive oil and mix well.
6. Transfer the mixture to the measuring cup.
7. Add the essential oils, if desired.
8. Pour into the small jar and label.
9. Store the salve in a cool, dark place for up to 9 months.

Magick Powders

Magick powders are easy to make with three main ingredients: ground-up herbs, essential oils, and glitter. Some Wiccans don't like to use glitter made of plastic, but there are eco-friendly alternatives made with biodegradable cellulose. Magick powders are sprinkled or blown into the air to release their power. Sprinkle them on your altar or on gifts, add them to spells, put them in your pocket or shoes, or roll spell candles in them.

Magick Blessing Powder

Sprinkle a little Blessing Powder to invoke the benediction of the Gods, purify your sacred space, enhance rituals and spells for dedication and consecration, and summon beneficial energies.

You will need:

- Mortar and pestle
- Dried herbs of your choice (gather as many as possible):

    | Clover | Lavender | Rose |
    | Elderberry | Myrrh | White sage |
    | Frankincense | | |

- Mason jar or container with lid
- Rose, lavender, and frankincense essential oils
- Blue and gold glitter (opt for non-plastic, eco-friendly glitter)
- Bottle with a cap

continued ▶

The Solitary Wiccan Apothecary 171

Magick Blessing Powder *continued*

1. Use the mortar and pestle to grind the herbs to a powdery consistency.

2. Transfer the powder into the jar. Add 1 drop of each of the essential oils and a dash of glitter. Be careful when adding the oils, as too much will make your powder sticky.

3. Seal the jar with an airtight lid and shake until the powder is well mixed. While you are shaking, be sure to concentrate on your intention.

4. Put your newly made magick powder in a bottle and label it.

Protection Powder

With the power of specially chosen protective herbs, you can create an impenetrable barrier against harm.

You will need:

- Mortar and pestle
- Dried herbs of your choice (gather as many as possible):

Anise	Dill	Mugwort
Basil	Garlic	Nettle
Bay leaf	Lavender	Rosemary
Black pepper	Marigold	Vervain
Cinnamon	Mint	

- Mason jar or container with lid
- Cedar and rose essential oils
- Silver glitter (opt for non-plastic, eco-friendly glitter)
- Bottle with a cap

1. Use the mortar and pestle to grind the herbs to a powder consistency.
2. Transfer the powder into the jar. Add 1 drop of each of the essential oils and a dash of glitter. Be careful when adding the oils, as too much will make your powder sticky.
3. Seal the jar with an airtight lid and shake until the powder is well mixed. While you are shaking, be sure to concentrate on your intention.
4. Put your newly made magick powder in a bottle and label it.

Winds of Change Powder

If things are going badly or you need a change of luck, whip up a batch of this powder to sweep away old, baneful energy and welcome in a fresh new tide of hope and joy.

You will need:

- Mortar and pestle

- Dried herbs of your choice (gather as many as possible):

Allspice	Lavender	Sage
Catnip	Lemon balm	Thyme
Ginger	Nutmeg	

- Mason jar or container with lid

- Vanilla essential oil

- Green glitter (opt for non-plastic, eco-friendly glitter)

- Bottle with a cap

1. Use the mortar and pestle to grind the herbs to a powder consistency.

2. Transfer the powder into the jar with a lid. Add 1 drop of essential oil and a dash of the glitter. Be careful when adding the oil, as too much will make your powder sticky.

3. Seal the jar with an airtight lid and shake until the powder is well mixed. While you are shaking, be sure to concentrate on your intention.

4. Put your newly made magick powder in a bottle and label it.

Wiccan Incense Recipes

Burning dried plants, sweet gums, resins, and woods is an ancient Wiccan practice used to strengthen the power of magick, ritual, and prayer. When you blend your incense, you change the vibration of the materials to correspond with your intention. As you are blending, be sure to keep your intention firmly in your mind and move your pestle in a clockwise direction. Use a mortar and pestle for easy crushing and blending. To use your incense, sprinkle it over a lit charcoal tablet in a small cauldron or heatproof dish.

Samhain Incense

Mix this blend on Samhain night and allow the smoke to carry your thoughts to loved ones beyond the veil.

You will need:

- ½ tablespoon cloves
- ½ tablespoon cinnamon
- 1½ tablespoons dried rosemary
- 1½ tablespoons dried apple leaf
- ½ tablespoon dragon's blood resin
- 5 drops patchouli oil

1. Use a mortar and pestle to crush the cloves, cinnamon, rosemary, apple leaf, and resin.
2. Add the essential oil and mix.
3. Store in an airtight container.

Yule Incense

Honor Yule with the scent of this sacred blend.

You will need:

- 2 tablespoons pine resin or dried needles
- 1 tablespoon dried juniper berries
- ½ cinnamon stick
- 1 tablespoon frankincense resin
- 5 drops cedar essential oil

1. Use a mortar and pestle to crush the needles, berries, cinnamon stick, and resin.
2. Add the essential oil and mix.
3. Store in an airtight container.

Imbolc Incense

Invoke the gentle birthing of spring with this blend's floral currents.

You will need:

- 2 tablespoons dried jasmine flowers
- 1 dried bay leaf
- Pinch of powdered milk
- 1 tablespoon myrrh resin
- 5 drops frankincense essential oil

1. Use a mortar and pestle to crush the flowers, bay leaf, powdered milk, and resin.
2. Add the essential oil and mix.
3. Store in an airtight container.

Ostara Incense

Spring has arrived! Burn this incense to celebrate Mother Earth's awakening.

You will need:

- 1 tablespoon dried orange peel
- 1 tablespoon ginger powder
- 1 tablespoon dried white sage
- 1 tablespoon dried rose petals
- 1 tablespoon myrrh resin
- 5 drops rose geranium essential oil

1. Use a mortar and pestle to crush the peel, spice, sage, petals, and resin.
2. Add the essential oil and mix.
3. Store in an airtight container.

Beltane Incense

Offer this incense gift at the sacred marriage of the Goddess and God.

You will need:

- 1 tablespoon red rose petals
- 1 tablespoon white rose petals
- 5 apple seeds
- 1 tablespoon dragon's blood resin
- 5 drops rose essential oil

1. Use a mortar and pestle to crush the petals, seeds, and resin.
2. Add the essential oil and mix.
3. Store in an airtight container.

The Solitary Wiccan Apothecary

Litha Incense

Burn this incense or throw it onto the Litha bonfire to honor the Sun God.

You will need:

- 1 tablespoon dried lavender
- 1 tablespoon dried chamomile flowers
- 1 tablespoon dried sunflower petals
- 1 tablespoon myrrh resin
- 5 drops lemon or sage essential oil

1. Use a mortar and pestle to crush the lavender, flowers, petals, and resin.
2. Add the essential oil and mix.
3. Store in an airtight container.

Lammas Incense

This meditative blend invites seasonal thanksgiving and gratitude.

You will need:

- 1 tablespoon dried chamomile flowers
- 1 tablespoon copal resin
- 2 tablespoons benzoin resin
- 5 drops lavender essential oil

1. Use a mortar and pestle to crush the flowers and resins.
2. Add the essential oil and mix.
3. Store in an airtight container.

Mabon Incense

Burn this autumnal incense as we spiral into the dark half of the year.

You will need:

- 1 tablespoon dried marigold petals
- 1 tablespoon dried sage
- 1 tablespoon dried blackberry leaves
- 1 tablespoon benzoin resin
- 5 drops myrrh essential oil

1. Use a mortar and pestle to crush the petals, sage, leaves, and resin.
2. Add the essential oil and mix.
3. Store in an airtight container.

Full Moon Incense

When the Moon is full, offer this special incense to the Mother Goddess.

You will need:

- 1 tablespoon dried jasmine
- 1 tablespoon dried poppy seeds
- 1 tablespoon dried lemon balm
- 1 tablespoon sandalwood chips
- 1 tablespoon myrrh resin
- 5 drops lemon essential oil

1. Use a mortar and pestle to crush the jasmine, seeds, balm, chips, and resin.
2. Add the essential oil and mix.
3. Store in an airtight container.

New Moon Incense

On the night of the New Moon, offer this incense to the Maiden Goddess.

You will need:

- 1 tablespoon dried chamomile flowers
- 1 tablespoon lemon balm
- 1 tablespoon sage
- 1 tablespoon camphor resin
- 5 drops myrrh essential oil

1. Use a mortar with a pestle to crush the flowers, lemon balm, sage, and resin.
2. Add the essential oil and mix.
3. Store in an airtight container.

Wiccan Magick Waters

Quite simply, magick water is water that has been charged by infusing it with herbs and crystals. Water can absorb and contain the vibrational energy of whatever is placed into it, creating a drinkable potion for magickal and ritual use. You can sprinkle the infused water around your home, sacred space, or workplace to bring it into alignment with the water's energetic properties. You can anoint yourself, dab it on spell or ritual ingredients, pour it into your bathwater, or even place a drop or two into your drinking water or ritual cup.

Psychic Powers Water

To enhance your psychic abilities, create this drinkable potion on the night of the New Moon and allow it to steep until the Moon is full.

You will need:

- 7 fresh or dried bay leaves
- 7 fresh or dried borage flowers
- 1 cinnamon stick
- 7 fresh or dried peppermint leaves
- 7 fresh or dried rowan berries
- 1 amethyst crystal
- 4-ounce glass jar with lid
- 4 ounces of Moon Water (page 108), spring water, or rainwater
- 4-ounce glass bottle (with an atomizer, if you prefer)

1. On the night of the New Moon, place the herbs and crystal in the jar.
2. Fill the jar with the water and seal.
3. Swirl the contents gently and visualize the soft purple light of clairvoyance filling it.
4. Place the jar on your altar and leave it undisturbed until the Full Moon.
5. On the night of the Full Moon, strain the water, pour it into the bottle, and label.
6. Hold your newly made potion to your Third Eye Chakra and once again visualize it filling with purple light.
7. When you are ready, say forcefully: *For the good of all and harm to none, this magick potion is now done!*

Happy Home Water

Spray, dab, or sprinkle this water everywhere baneful energy is lurking to bring peace and joy back into your space.

You will need:

- 9 fresh or dried jasmine flowers
- 1 tablespoon fresh or dried catnip
- 1 tablespoon fresh or dried lavender flowers
- 1 tablespoon fresh or dried chamomile flowers
- 7 fresh or dried violet or pansy flowers
- 1 rose quartz crystal
- 4-ounce glass jar with lid
- 4 ounces of Moon Water (page 108), spring water, or rainwater
- 4-ounce glass bottle (with an atomizer, if you prefer)

1. On the night of the New Moon, place the herbs and crystal in the jar.
2. Fill the jar with the water and seal.
3. Swirl the contents gently, envisioning it filling up with the soft pink light of happiness.
4. Place the jar on your altar and leave it undisturbed until the Full Moon.
5. On the night of the Full Moon, strain the water, pour it into the bottle, and label.
6. Hold your newly made potion to your Heart Chakra and envision the liquid filled with the pink light of happiness.
7. When you are ready, say forcefully: *For the good of all and harm to none, this magick potion is now done!*

Clear Quartz Gemstone Elixir

A gemstone elixir is created by placing a crystal into water. The energy, power, and vibrations of the crystal permeate the liquid, creating a potion. You can drink the elixir (approximately 7 drops, 3 times a day), add it to your bathwater or watering can, or anoint your body with it. Clear quartz promotes healing, protection, and cleansing. Make this on a sunny day, as sunlight helps activate the potion.

You will need:

- 1 clear quartz crystal
- A spoon
- 1 cup water
- 1-pint mason jar with lid
- Cheesecloth
- 1-quart mason jar with lid
- ½ cup vinegar

1. First, cleanse your crystal by doing one of the following:
   - smudge with Palo Santo or incense
   - bury in a bowl of sea salt or earth overnight
   - hold it under running water until it feels clean
   - cleanse it with a soft cloth that has been dipped into Moon Water
   - leave it overnight in the light of the Full Moon
   - leave it for several hours in bright sunlight

2. Once your crystal is cleansed, don't touch it with your bare hands; use the spoon to move it so it doesn't absorb your personal energy.

3. Be sure you are in a calm and focused emotional state when making your elixir.

continued ▶

Clear Quartz Gemstone Elixir *continued*

4. Set your intention with mindful visualization by seeing the finished elixir brimming and sparkling with positive, protective, healing vibrations.

5. Put the water in the 1-pint mason jar. Use the spoon to add the crystal.

6. Cover the jar with the cheesecloth and place it outside in the sunlight for a couple of hours.

7. Use the spoon to remove the crystal. Pour the elixir into the 1-quart mason jar.

8. Add the vinegar to preserve the elixir and fix the vibration.

9. Label your newly made gemstone elixir with the name and date.

Four Thieves Vinegar

Four Thieves vinegar is a hex-breaking, banishing, and warding concoction thought to have originated during medieval times. It has a pleasant taste and can be used as a salad dressing and sprinkled on veggies, and it's also an excellent banishing potion. Begin making this on the night of the Full Moon and finish it at the Dark Moon so you may take advantage of the decreasing, banishing Moon tide.

You will need:

- ¼ cup rosemary
- ¼ cup sage
- ¼ cup lavender flowers
- ¼ cup thyme
- ¼ cup mint
- 3 garlic cloves
- 2 cups apple cider vinegar
- 2 (1-quart) mason jars with lids
- A strainer
- Cheesecloth

1. Remove leaves and flowers from the stems.
2. Chop the garlic roughly.
3. Place the herbs and garlic in the mason jar.
4. Cover with the vinegar and seal tightly.
5. Label and date your potion.
6. Store in a cool, dry place. Shake gently once a day until the night of the Dark Moon.
7. On the night of the Dark Moon, strain the vinegar into a clean mason jar and discard the herbs.

Ways to Use Four Thieves Vinegar

Sprinkle on your doorstep, home, altar, or sacred space to ward off unwelcome energies.

Add to food as a protective potion.

Put in a spray bottle and spritz around your home to banish unwanted energies.

Add to bathwater for protection and to ward off unwanted energy.

Drink a tablespoon to ward off illness.

Place some on a clean cloth and use it to cleanse your altar and tools of magick.

Anoint your body for protection.

Dab some on spell candles used for banishing, warding, and protection.

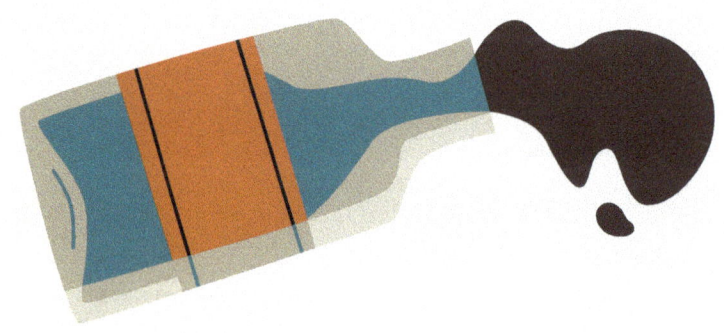

Charm Bags and Sachets

A charm bag is a spell enclosed in a bag. You can put it in your pocket or purse, place it in your car, or give it to a friend or family member when they need an extra boost of charmed energy.

Love Charm Bag

Try making this practical love charm to increase your animal magnetism and turn up your fascinating allure. It's filled with a blend of magickal herbs, flowers, crystals, and resins chosen to attract love.

You will need:

- 6-inch square of red fabric and 8 inches of red ribbon, or a red drawstring bag
- 3 candy hearts
- Rose quartz crystal
- Pinch of cinnamon
- Pinch of cloves
- Pinch of dragon's blood resin
- Pinch of ginger
- 3 dried red rosebuds
- 7 drops rose or rose geranium essential oil

1. Place the ingredients in the center of the cloth or put them in the bag.
2. As you add each component, visualize yourself loved in the way you desire and send your intention out into the Universe.
3. If using fabric, tie it closed with the ribbon; if using a bag, pull it closed with the drawstrings.
4. As you tie or pull, use a firm hand and state: *It is done!*
5. Keep the bag with you as much as possible and sleep with it under your pillow at night.

Money Charm Bag

Want to increase your wealth and prosperity? Make this charm bag that will draw money to you. It's filled with a blend of magickal herbs, flowers, and crystals chosen to bring cash quickly.

You will need:

- 6-inch square of green fabric and 8 inches of green ribbon, or a green drawstring bag
- 3 coins
- Citrine crystal
- Pinches of dried mint, allspice, and basil
- 3 dried clover flowers
- 12 drops of Money Oil (put 7 drops basil essential oil, 7 drops clove essential oil, and 1 drop ginger essential oil in a 5 ml glass vial, fill with base oil [page 158], and cap the vial)

1. Place the ingredients in the center of the cloth or put them in the bag.
2. As you add each component, visualize yourself as a wealthy and prosperous person and send your intention out into the Universe.
3. If using fabric, tie it closed with ribbon; if using a bag, pull it closed with the drawstrings.
4. As you tie or pull, use a firm hand and state: *It is done!*
5. Keep the bag with you as much as possible and sleep with it under your pillow at night.

Divination Sachet

A sachet is a bag that has been filled with herbs and flowers and sewn together. The bag can be cut into any shape, but a square bag is easiest to make. The most significant difference between a sachet and a charm bag is that sachets are to be worn around the neck when you're using them. Wear this sachet whenever you are doing any divination work. To activate, squeeze the sachet gently to release the magick.

You will need:

- Purple or dark blue fabric
- A needle and thread
- Mortar and pestle
- Pinch of cinnamon
- 1 tablespoon dried mugwort
- 1 tablespoon dried marigold petals
- 1 whole star anise
- 1 tablespoon dried borage flower
- 5 drops lemongrass essential oil
- 30 inches of purple or dark blue ribbon

1. On the night of the New Moon, cut two 4-inch squares of fabric.

2. Sew three edges of the fabric together, leaving one side open. As you stitch, keep in mind that your needle is directing energy into the material. Each time it pierces it and each loop that binds the fabric seals your intention.

3. Use the mortar and pestle to crush the herbs and flowers. Be sure to move your pestle in a clockwise direction to draw positive energy.

continued ▶

Divination Sachet *continued*

4. When the herbs are finely crushed, hold the mortar up to the moonlight and chant:

   New Moon power, New Moon night,

   Psychic herbs will bring to light

   All that I shall want to know,

   By my will, I make it so!

5. Carefully pour the herbs into the sachet.

6. Sprinkle 5 drops of essential oil into the sachet.

7. Sew the top of the sachet closed and attach the ribbon to each side to form a loop.

8. Hold the completed sachet to your Heart Chakra while envisioning yourself as competent and accomplished in the art of divination. Take your time with this step; concentrate as strongly as possible.

9. When you are ready, seal the charge by drawing an Earth-invoking Pentagram in the air over your sachet using your athame, wand, or the first two fingers of your power hand.

Earth-invoking Pentagram

Beeswax Sabbat Candles

Make your own Sabbat candles with sheets of beeswax, herbs, and essential oils. Rolled beeswax candles are simple to make and have a beautiful scent when burned. The addition of herbs and essential oils in the rolling process will create specially charged candles for each Sabbat.

Use the following method for making all your candles:

1. You will need a very sharp or X-ACTO knife, a wick, and a sturdy cutting surface.

2. Beeswax usually comes in 8-by-16-inch sheets, so cut each sheet in half lengthwise for an 8-inch candle.

3. Before you begin, be sure your wax sheet is malleable; if it's too cold, it will crack and be difficult to roll. After cutting the sheet in half, warm it gently with a blow-dryer set to the lowest heat setting. Be careful; you don't want to melt your wax.

4. Cut the wick about 2 inches longer than the wax.

5. Use a mortar and pestle to grind the herbs to a fine powder.

6. Sprinkle the herbs and essential oils onto the wax sheet.

7. Place the wick along the edge of the wax sheet and carefully bend the wax over the wick; be sure the wick is tight in the wax and press firmly.

8. Roll the candle slowly, keeping it as straight as possible with the ends even. Keep thoughts of the Sabbat firmly in your mind.

9. If you won't be using the candles immediately, wrap them in tissue, label, and store in a cool, dry place.

Samhain Candles

Invoke the spirit of Samhain with these scented candles that are empowered by the light of your intention and the heat of your hands.

You will need:

- Orange and/or black wax sheets
- Pinch of one or more herbs:

Angelica	Mugwort	Wormwood
Catnip	Rosemary	
Heather	Witch hazel	

- 3 drops each: cinnamon, sage, and ginger essential oils
- Prepare using the method on page 191.

Yule Candles

Add some Yuletide cheer to your altar, sacred space, or home with these seasonally inspired candles.

You will need:

- Red and/or green wax sheets
- Pinch of one or more herbs:

Cedar	Rosemary
Pine	Sage

- 3 drops each: frankincense, myrrh, and pine essential oils
- Prepare using the method on page 191.

Imbolc Candles

White is the color of the Maiden Goddess, who is honored at Imbolc. The flames of your handmade candles shall be a beacon of hope and light.

You will need:

- White wax sheets
- Pinch of one or more herbs:
    - Angelica
    - Basil
    - Blackberry
    - Heather
    - Jasmine
    - Violets
- 3 drops each: jasmine, camphor, and myrrh essential oils
- Prepare using the method on page 191.

Ostara Candles

The fiery scent of these pretty pastel candles will be sure to help you attune with the awakening energy of Mother Earth.

You will need:

- Pastel wax sheets
- Pinch of one or more herbs:
    - Cinquefoil
    - Dandelion
    - Honeysuckle
    - Jasmine
    - Rose
    - Violet
- 3 drops each: orange, ginger, and sage essential oils
- Prepare using the method on page 191.

Beltane Candles

Red and white candles with a swooning floral scent shall put you in the mood for a springtime celebration! As the saying goes, *"White is for the lady fair, white for her groom and the love they share."*

You will need:

- Red and/or white wax sheets
- Pinch of one or more herbs:

Angelica	Honeysuckle	Marigold
Blackberry	Lilac	Woodruff

- 4 drops each: jasmine and rose essential oil
- Prepare using the method on page 191.

Litha Candles

Midsummer magick is in the air. When you burn these candles, you may just spy a faerie or pixie through the flames.

You will need:

- Gold and/or red wax sheets
- Pinch of one or more herbs:

Chamomile	Honeysuckle	Thyme
Fern	Lavender	Vervain
Heliotrope	St. John's wort	

- 3 drops each: lavender, rose, and lemon essential oils
- Prepare using the method on page 191.

Lammas Candles

The easy days of summer are captured in the color and scent of these Sabbat candles.

You will need:

- Green and/or yellow wax sheets
- Pinch of one or more herbs:
    - Calendula
    - Corn silk
    - Heather
    - Hollyhock
    - Oakleaf
    - Sunflower
- 3 drops each: chamomile, rosemary, and frankincense essential oils
- Prepare using the method on page 191.

Mabon Candles

As the Earth prepares for winter, take a walk through an old growth forest with the evocative earthy scent and color of your Mabon candles.

You will need:

- Maroon and/or gold wax sheets
- Pinch of one or more herbs:
    - Blackberry
    - Cedar
    - Marigold
    - Pumpkin seed
    - Sage
- 3 drops each: cedar, myrrh, and pine essential oils
- Prepare using the method on page 191.

Beeswax Healing Poppet

A poppet is a type of image magick in the form of a human figure that represents a specific person. Poppet magick is as old as witchcraft, and poppets are used for lots of different magickal purposes. Beeswax poppets are particularly satisfying to work with because the wax softens at body temperature and is easily malleable.

You will need:

- 1 green or natural beeswax sheet
- ½ teaspoon of one or more of the following herbs, finely ground with a mortar and pestle:

Bay leaf	Heliotrope	Pine
Cedar	Lemon balm	Rose
Cinnamon	Mint	Rosemary
Fennel	Nettle	Vervain

- A candle-carving tool (a nutpick, pushpin, or metal skewer works well)

1. On the night of the Full Moon, gather all the ingredients.
2. Melt the wax in a double boiler or in a metal bowl over hot water.
3. Remove the bowl from the hot water and allow the wax to cool enough that you can handle it.
4. Scoop the wax into your hands and sprinkle the herbs onto it. The warmth of your hands will keep the wax soft enough for working.
5. Begin to shape the wax into a human figure. It doesn't have to be a work of art; a rudimentary shape with a body, head, arms, and legs will do.

6. As you're shaping the wax, visualize healing energy flowing into it and chant:

    Melted beeswax, herbs, and flowers

    Fills this poppet with healing powers.

7. Once you're happy with the shape of your wax, use the candle-carving tool to inscribe the name of the person to be healed, the date, and the healing rune Sowulo into the wax figure.

8. While you are inscribing, chant:

    Healing poppet magick flows,

    Health returns, illness goes.

Sowulo Rune

9. Hold the completed poppet to your Heart Chakra and chant three times three (nine times):

    Heal [name] now, o little one,

    For the highest good and harm to none!

10. Keep the poppet on your altar until you feel healing is complete or the poppet is no longer needed.

11. Deconstruct the poppet by melting it in a double boiler and disposing of the wax.

Drinkable Elements Potions

Transform ordinary tap water into a magick potion by charging it with colored light, enchanting it, and letting it sit within natural sunlight for a few hours' time. In addition to being consumed, these potions can be sprinkled on anything to impart their Elemental powers. If you can't find the correct color of glass, paint the outside of a clear glass bottle with nontoxic paint. Be sure to use a funnel when adding the water so none of the paint gets into the container.

Element of Air Potion

Sip a small amount of Air Element Potion before working with the Element and sprinkle the potion in the Eastern quarter of your Circle.

You will need:

- 1 yellow glass bottle with cap
- 1 sprig of fresh peppermint

1. Fill the yellow bottle with clear water; as you pour, be mindful of the Element of Air and say: *Water into Air, blessed be!*
2. Add the peppermint and cap the bottle.
3. Swirl the liquid several times and set it on a sunny window ledge.
4. Strain, rebottle, and cap the liquid.

Element of Fire Potion

Sip a small amount of Fire Element Potion before working with the Element and sprinkle the potion in the Southern quarter of your Circle.

You will need:

- 1 red glass bottle with cap
- 1 sprig of fresh basil

1. Fill the red bottle with clear water; as you pour, be mindful of the Element of Fire and say: *Water into Fire, blessed be!*
2. Add the basil and cap the bottle.
3. Swirl the liquid several times and set it on a sunny window ledge.
4. Strain, rebottle, and cap the liquid.

Element of Water Potion

Sip a small amount of Water Element Potion before working with the Element and sprinkle the potion in the Western quarter of your Circle.

You will need:

- 1 blue glass bottle with cap
- 1 sprig of fresh thyme

1. Fill the blue bottle with clear water; as you pour, be mindful of the Element of Water and say: *Water into Water, blessed be!*
2. Add the thyme and cap the bottle.
3. Swirl the liquid several times and set it on a sunny window ledge.
4. Strain, rebottle, and cap the liquid.

Earth Element Potion

Sip a small amount of Earth Element Potion before working with the Element and sprinkle the potion in the Northern quarter of your Circle.

You will need:

- 1 green glass bottle with cap
- 1 sprig of fresh sage

1. Fill the green bottle with clear water; as you pour, be mindful of the Element of Earth and say: *Water into Earth, blessed be!*
2. Add the sage and cap the bottle.
3. Swirl the liquid several times and set it on a sunny window ledge.
4. Strain, rebottle, and cap the liquid.

Smudge Sticks

Smudging is the art of altering vibrations using the smoke of sacred herbs. Using a feather or a fan, waft the smoke around the room or toward the person or object to be cleansed.

You will need:

- Garden clippers
- Plant branches from one or more of the following herbs:
  - Cedar: healing, purification, protection
  - Lavender: purification, protection, peace
  - Mugwort: protection, healing
  - Pine: protection, banishing spirits, healing
  - Rosemary: protection, exorcism, purification
  - Sage: protection, wisdom
  - Sweetgrass: calling in Spirits
- Scissors
- String

1. Cut small branches of the plant 6 to 10 inches in length.
2. Using scissors, cut string three times the length of the branches.
3. Use one end of the string to tie the stems tightly. Wrap the string around the branches from the stem to the top; be sure to pull the string tightly and wrap firmly.
4. Once you reach the top of the branches, reverse direction and wrap the string back down to the bottom stem and tie it off.
5. On a flat surface, gently roll your smudge stick into a uniform shape.
6. Cut off any straggly bits and trim the top flat for easier lighting.
7. Place the smudge stick in a wicker basket or on a wire rack to dry.

Dark Moon Witch's Salt

Black salt is used for protection, banishing, and breaking hexes. Use it in spells, rituals, sachets, incense, and spell bags for uncrossing, hex removal, and bindings. A pinch under your pillow will prevent bad dreams, and a sprinkle on your doorstep will stop harmful energy from entering your home. Carried on your person, it will ward off bullying, gossip, and rudeness. To dispose of it, bury it in the Earth or cast it into the wind, running water, or a fire.

You will need:

- A charcoal disc
- A lighter or matches
- Candle snuffer
- A black cast iron cauldron
- 1 tablespoon each of 3 of the following herbs of your choice (3 tablespoons in total):

Basil	Mugwort	Rosemary
Clove	Nettle	Juniper
Mint	Pine Needles	Thistle

- A spoon
- Mortar and pestle
- 8 tablespoons sea salt
- A black candle
- A white plate
- Patchouli essential oil
- A container with lid

1. At the Dark Moon (the night before New Moon), light the charcoal disc and place it in the cauldron.
2. Add the herbs and allow everything to burn down to ash, including the charcoal disc.
3. Scrape the inside of the cauldron with the spoon and transfer the scrapings into the mortar.
4. Moving the pestle counterclockwise (for banishing), crush the scrapings into a fine powder while chanting:

Salt and herbs at Dark Moon night

Shall banish baneful from my sight.

5. Mix in the salt.
6. Light the candle and hold the plate over the flame to collect the candle smoke's soot.
7. When the plate is black, scrape the soot into the mortar and mix.
8. Add 3 drops of essential oil and mix three times three (nine times) while chanting:

Salt and oil, coal and soot,

Dark Moon banishing is afoot!

9. Transfer to a container, seal tightly, and label.

GO YE HAPPY SOLITARY WAY

We've walked together through the pages of this book, and now we must part ways. For you who are new to Wicca, I hope this book is helpful and answers some of your questions. We've explored the origins and tenets of the Wiccan faith that will ground you to your practice. You have touched on the guideposts of our Wiccan belief that will light your way: balance in all things, tolerance, humility, and harmony with the natural world.

As you continue your Wiccan path, I hope you will move forward with confidence and reverence to experience personal and spiritual growth through a deeper understanding of the beautiful faith called Wicca. Together we have made magick, honored the Wheel of the Year, worshipped under the light of the Full Moon, and crafted traditions and celebrations that speak truthfully to your authentic Solitary Wiccan soul. Trust the Goddess and your intuition, remember to follow your heart and spirit, and believe in the power that shines within you!

Remember it's up to you to decide which way to go and how to get there. There is no wrong path to the Divine Spirit. Embrace the sacredness of the Earth, Moon, Sun, and stars and the lessons they can teach you. Continue to learn, experiment, and grow with joy and reverence.

May the Gods bless and guide you on your Solitary Path!

RESOURCES

***Buckland's Complete Book of Witchcraft* by Raymond Buckland** (Llewellyn Publications, 2002)

This book is often referred to as Uncle Bucky's big blue book. Raymond Buckland is one of the Elders of modern Wicca, and his book is a complete and comprehensive guide.

***Cunningham's Encyclopedia of Magical Herbs* by Scott Cunningham** (Llewellyn Publications, 2000)

One of my go-to books for everything herbal.

***The Element Encyclopedia of 5,000 Spells* by Judika Illes** (Element, 2004)

This is an excellent resource for spells, incantations, potions, and charms for every occasion and intention.

***The Elements of Ritual* by Deborah Lipp** (Llewellyn Publications, 2003)

An in-depth view of the art of creating ritual.

***The Goddess Path* by Patricia Monaghan** (Llewellyn Publications, 1999)

This book explores Goddesses from many different cultures.

***The Inner Temple of Witchcraft* by Christopher Penczak** (Llewellyn Publications, 2002)

A comprehensive guide that presents the history, traditions, and principles of Witchcraft and Wicca.

LearnReligions.com/paganism-wicca-4684806

A very informative website that answers just about any question you can imagine about Wicca in an informative and easy to understand manner.

***Llewellyn's Complete Book of Correspondences* by Sandra Kynes** (Llewellyn Publications, 2013)

A complete and comprehensive guide to magickal correspondences and a very handy asset for those who want to create their own spells.

***Modern Wicca* by Rowan Morgana** (Rockridge Press, 2020)

A guide to beliefs and traditions for the contemporary Wiccan.

***Moon Magick* by D.J Conway** (Llewellyn Publications, 2002)

Everything you need to know about the Moon is included in this book. A wealth of spells, rituals, and lore.

***Philosophy of Wicca* by Amber Laine Fisher** (ECW Press, 2002)

This beautifully written book explores ways and means of building personal faith and connecting with the Goddess.

***Real Magic* by Isaac Bonewits** (Red Wheel/Weiser, 1989)

This book explores the laws of magick written by an expert who graduated from University of California, Berkeley, in 1970 with a bachelor's degree in magic and thaumaturgy.

SacredWicca.com

Rowan Morgana's website with tons of free information and original rituals and spells.

***Seasons of Witchery* by Ellen Duggan** (Llewellyn Publications, 2012)

A guide to magickal practices throughout the Wheel of the Year.

***Sisters of the Dark Moon* by Gail Wood** (Llewellyn Publications, 2001)

A guide to creating Dark Moon rituals throughout the year.

***A Victorian Grimoire* by Patricia Telesco** (Llewellyn Publications, 1992)

A delight that is filled with Victorian-era magickal treasures.

***Wiccan Meditations* by Laura Wildman** (Citadel, 2002)

A how-to book on meditation and trancework with some lovely meditations.

***The Witch in Every Woman* by Laurie Cabot** (Delta, 1997)

A book of empowerment for women who wish to reclaim their sovereignty.

***The Witch's Familiar* by Raven Grimassi** (Llewellyn Publications, 2003)

Everything you ever wanted or needed to know about familiars, both physical and spirit!

***Witchcraft for Tomorrow* by Doreen Valiente** (Robert Hale, 1993)

A basic overview of Wicca from someone who was there from the beginning! It's an excellent resource for learning more about Wiccan history and lore and has some great poetry and spells.

***A Witch's Beverages and Brews* by Patricia Telesco** (Weiser, 2009)

Teaches how to make and drink ritual beverages, potions, and brews.

***A Witches' Bible* by Janet & Stewart Farrar** (Phoenix Publishing Inc, 1996)

This fascinating book by initiates of the Gardnerian Tradition reveals their spells, rituals, and lore.

GLOSSARY

archetypes: Images or prototypes of universal ideals

affirmation: The practice of positive thinking

amulet: A protective object that is worn or carried

animism: The belief that everything has a soul

baneful: Something that is harmful

binding: A spell that prevents or restricts

Blue Moon: Occurs when there are two Full Moons in a month; the second Moon is the Blue Moon

calling the quarters: To summon the Elemental energies into the magick Circle

centering: To gather energy together to focus it on an intention

charge: To program an object toward a specific purpose

chakras: 7 major energy centers located within the physical body

collective energy: A shared consciousness

consecration: The act of making something sacred

cleansing: Purifying an object of baneful or unwanted energy

correspondences: Specific magickal properties and energies

craft: A short term for witchcraft

Dark Moon: Occurs the night before the New Moon

dressing oil: A specially prepared oil applied to magickal objects before a spell or ritual used to add a magickal charge

elder: A person who has a vast knowledge of Wicca and has made an impact on the Wiccan community

elemental spirit: A spirit that is associated with one of the four Elements of Earth, Air, Fire, and Water

Esbat: A Wiccan gathering to honor the Moon and to work magick; Esbats occur on Full Moons, New Moons, or Dark Moons

Full Moon: The monthly cycle when the entire Moon is visible from the Earth

grounding: To become aware of and connected with the Earth

incantation: Recited words as part of a spell or the words that are the spell

intent: The real purpose of the magick at hand; the goal of the spell or ritual

invoke: To draw a spirit to your body such as Drawing Down the Moon or Sun

Moon Water: Sacred water that has been charged by the light of the Moon

Law of Attraction: Positive or negative thoughts will bring positive or negative experiences

Law of Three: Whatever energy sent out into the world returns three-fold to the sender

New Moon: The first phase of the Moon; the beginning of the monthly Moon cycle

pantheist: The belief that God, Goddess is in everything that exists

pantheon: A group of Gods of a particular mythology

Patron God, Goddess: A personal guide or protector

petitions: An intent or desire that is ritually created and used as a stand-alone spell or as part of a more extensive working

polytheism: The belief that there are many Gods

power hand: Your most magickally attuned hand, and often your dominant hand in daily life use

purification: To remove unwanted, baneful energies or influences

resin: A natural incense made from tree or plant sap

raising energy: Gathering power to use in magickal workings

Sabbat: The eight witches' holidays that celebrate the Turning of the Wheel

sachet: A cloth bag containing herbs, crystals, petitions, and charms that is worn or carried for magickal purposes

shamanic: A spiritual healing practice that involves trance work

sigil: A magickal symbol used in spells

smudge: A bundle of smoldering herbs or burning incense used to purify or bless an object or space

sympathetic magick: Symbolically imitating a person, place, or thing to gain influence over it

talisman: A charm that is worn or carried to ward off baneful energy

Turning of the Wheel: The progression of the seasons

Threefold Law: See Law of Three

underworld: The realm of the dead or the spirit world

visualization: The practice of using the power of your mind to create change

ward: Protection or guardian, whether spiritual, magickal, or physical

Wheel of the Year: The Wiccan cycle of seasonal festivals called Sabbats

will: Your correct path in alignment with your purpose in the Universe

SPELL INDEX

A
Attract Love Tea, 139
Autumn Count Your Blessings Spell, 77–78

B
Banishing Potion Spell, 151
Banishing Tea, 140
Beeswax Healing Poppet, 196–197
Beltane Candles, 194
Beltane Incense, 177
Beltane Sabbat Oil, 163
Beltane Sabbat Ritual, 95–97
Brigid's Imbolc Custard, 125–126

C
Candied Flowers, 148–150
Cast Your Singular Circle, 44–45
Chocolate Mousse for Happiness Spell, 146–147
Cleansing Bath for Purification, 62
Clear Quartz Gemstone Elixir, 183–184
Courage Tea, 140
The Crystal Pentagram Spell, 69–70
Cupid's Carrot Cake, 131

D
Dark Moon Witch's Salt, 202–203
Divination Sachet, 189–190
Divination Tea, 141

E
Early Spring Spell of Hope, 73–74
Earth Element Potion, 200
Elemental Ritual, 106–107
Element of Air Potion, 198
Element of Fire Potion, 199
Element of Water Potion, 199

F
Following the Path Honey Jar Spell, 47–48
Four Thieves Vinegar, 185–186
Full Moon Incense, 179

G
Greenman Wild Nettle Soup, 154

H
Happiness Tea, 142
Happy Home Water, 182
Healing Tea, 141
Hecate's Key Spell, 59–61
Honey Rose Elixir, 144

I
Imbolc Candles, 193
Imbolc Incense, 176
Imbolc Sabbat Oil, 161
Imbolc Sabbat Ritual, 91–92

L
Lammas Bread Magick, 134–135
Lammas Candles, 195
Lammas Incense, 178
Lammas Sabbat Oil, 164
Lammas Sabbat Ritual, 100–101
Lavender Lemonade, 145
Lavender Sugar, 129
Litha Candles, 194
Litha Fire Cider Tonic, 132–133
Litha Incense, 178
Litha Midsummer Sabbat Ritual, 98–99

Litha Sabbat Oil, 164
Love Charm Bag, 187
Lucky Tea, 143

M

Mabon Apple Cake, 136–137
Mabon Candles, 196
Mabon Incense, 179
Mabon Sabbat Oil, 166
Mabon Sabbat Ritual, 102–103
Mabon Wishes Applesauce, 138
Magick Blessing Powder, 171–172
Money Charm Bag, 188
Morning Ritual, 84–85

N

New Moon Incense, 180
New Moon Letters to the Goddess, 66–68
New Moon Out with the Old, In with the New Spell, 52–53
New Moon Ritual of Artemis, 115–117

O

Ostara Candles, 193
Ostara Incense, 177
Ostara Magick Eggs, 127–128
Ostara Sabbat Oil, 162
Ostara Sabbat Ritual, 93–94

P

Plant Familiar Ritual, 112–114
Prosperity Meditation Spell, 71–72
Prosperity Tea, 143
Protection Powder, 173
Protection Salve, 170
Protection Tea, 143
Psychic Powers Water, 181

R

Release Your Singular Circle, 46
Ritual of Dedication, 19–20

The River of Love Ritual, 110–111
Rosebud Love Salve, 169

S

Samhain Candles, 192
Samhain Incense, 175
Samhain Sabbat Oil, 159
Samhain Sabbat Ritual, 86–87
Samhain Soul Cakes, 120–121
Self-Love Affirmation Spell, 54–55
Simple Syrups for Magick, 152–153
Smudge Sticks, 201
Solitary Full Moon Esbat Ritual, 108–109
A Solitary Spell for Self-Healing, 63–65
Spell to Draw Like-Minded People, 56–58
Spell to Strengthen Magikal Power, 49–51
Strawberry Jam Love Spell, 130
Summer Spell of Courage, 75–76

W

Wiccan Dream Salve, 167–168
Winds of Change Powder, 174
Winter Protection Spell: A Witch's Bottle, 79–81
The Witch's Pyramid Ritual, 104–105

Y

Yule Candles, 192
Yule Gingerbread Magick Charm Cookies, 122–124
Yule Incense, 175
Yule Sabbat Oil, 160
Yule Sabbat Ritual, 88–90

INDEX

A
Affirmations, 54
Air element, 16
    Element of Air Potion, 198
Altars, 29
Aphrodite, 14
April Wind Moon, 38
Artemis, 115–117
Athames, 24
August Corn Moon, 39

B
Banishing
    Banishing Potion Spell, 151
    Banishing Tea, 140
    Four Thieves Vinegar, 185–186
Basil, 27
Beltane, 35, 129
    Beltane Candles, 194
    Beltane Incense, 177
    Beltane Sabbat Oil, 163
    Beltane Sabbat Ritual, 95–97
    Lavender Sugar, 129
    Strawberry Jam Love Spell, 130, 131
Blessing, 171–172
Brigid, 14, 125–126

C
Candles, 24, 191
    Beltane Candles, 194
    Imbolc Candles, 193
    Lammas Candles, 195
    Litha Candles, 194
    Mabon Candles, 196
    Ostara Candles, 193
    Samhain Candles, 192
    Yule Candles, 192
Catnip, 27
Chalices, 24
Circles
    casting, 44–45
    releasing, 46
Cleansing, 32, 62
Consecration, 32
Correspondences, 15
Country Wiccans, 4–5
Crone Goddess, 11–12, 59–61
Crystals, 24
Cups, 24

D
December Long Nights Moon, 40
Dedication, 18–20
Deities, 10–14
Diana, 13
Divination
    Divination Sachet, 189–190
    Divination Tea, 141
Divine energy, 15
Dreams, 167–168

E
Earth element, 17
    Earth Element Potion, 200
Elements, 16–17, 106–107
Empowering, 33
Energy, 3–4, 10, 15
Esbats, 37–40
Essential oils, 28
Eucalyptus, 28

F

Familiars, 112–114
February Quickening Moon, 37
Fire element, 16–17
    Element of Fire Potion, 199
Flora, 14
Flowers, 148–150
Frankincense, 28
Fruits, 152–153

G

Gardner, Gerald, 2
Goddesses, 11–14
    Brigid's Imbolc Custard, 125–126
    Hecate's Key Spell, 59–61
    New Moon Letters to the Goddess, 66–68
    New Moon Ritual of Artemis, 115–117
Gods, 10
Greenman, 154

H

Happiness
    Chocolate Mousse for Happiness Spell, 146–147
    Happiness Tea, 142
    Happy Home Water, 182
    Lavender Lemonade, 145
Healing
    Beeswax Healing Poppet, 196–197
    Healing Tea, 141
    Honey Rose Elixir, 144
    A Solitary Spell for Self-Healing, 63–65
Hecate, 13, 59–61
Herbs, 26–27
Home, 182

I

Imbolc, 35
    Brigid's Imbolc Custard, 125–126
    Imbolc Candles, 193
    Imbolc Incense, 176
    Imbolc Sabbat Oil, 161
    Imbolc Sabbat Ritual, 91–92
Incense, 25, 175
    Beltane Incense, 177
    Full Moon Incense, 179
    Imbolc Incense, 176
    Lammas Incense, 178
    Litha Incense, 178
    Mabon Incense, 179
    New Moon Incense, 180
    Ostara Incense, 177
    Samhain Incense, 175
    Yule Incense, 175
Isis, 13

J

January Cold Moon, 37
Jasmine, 28
July Blessing Moon, 39
June Strong Sun Moon, 38

K

Keys, 59–61
Knives, 24

L

Lammas, 36
    Lammas, 100–101
    Lammas Bread Magick, 134–135
    Lammas Candles, 195
    Lammas Incense, 178
    Lammas Sabbat Oil, 164
Lavender, 26
Law of Attraction, 7

Law of Three, 7
Lemongrass, 28
Litha, 36
    Litha Candles, 194
    Litha Fire Cider Tonic, 132–133
    Litha Incense, 178
    Litha Midsummer Sabbat Ritual, 98–99
    Litha Sabbat Oil, 164
Love
    Attract Love Tea, 139
    Honey Rose Elixir, 144
    Lavender Lemonade, 145
    Love Charm Bag, 187
    The River of Love Ritual, 110–111
    Rosebud Love Salve, 169
    Self-Love Affirmation Spell, 54–55
    Strawberry Jam Love Spell, 130
Luck
    Lucky Tea, 143
    Winds of Change Powder, 174

M

Mabon, 36, 136
    Mabon, 102–103
    Mabon Apple Cake, 136–137
    Mabon Candles, 196
    Mabon Incense, 179
    Mabon Sabbat Oil, 166
    Mabon Wishes Applesauce, 138
Magickal shapes, 124
Magick waters, 180
    Clear Quartz Gemstone Elixir, 183–184
    Happy Home Water, 182
    Psychic Powers Water, 181

Maiden Goddess, 11
March Storm Moon, 37
May Flower Moon, 38
Meditations, 71–72
Moons, 37–40
    Dark Moon Witch's Salt, 202–203
    Full Moon Incense, 179
    New Moon Incense, 180
    New Moon Letters to the Goddess, 66–68
    New Moon Out with the Old, In with the New Spell, 52–53
    New Moon Ritual of Artemis, 115–117
    Solitary Full Moon Esbat Ritual, 108–109
Mother Goddess, 11

N

Natural dyes, 128
Nature, 110–111
November Mourning Moon, 40

O

October Blood Moon, 40
Oils, 158
    Beltane Sabbat Oil, 163
    Imbolc Sabbat Oil, 161
    Lammas Sabbat Oil, 164
    Litha Sabbat Oil, 164
    Mabon Sabbat Oil, 166
    Ostara Sabbat Oil, 162
    Samhain Sabbat Oil, 159
    Yule Sabbat Oil, 160
Ostara, 35
    Ostara Candles, 193
    Ostara Incense, 177

Ostara Magick Eggs, 127–128
Ostara Sabbat Oil, 162
Ostara Sabbat Ritual, 93–94

P

Palo Santo, 27
Patchouli, 28
Patron Gods, 10
Pentagrams, 69–70
Peppermint, 26
Personal power, 15, 21, 49–51
Positivity, 7
Powders, 171
    Magick Blessing Powder, 171–172
    Protection Powder, 173
    Winds of Change Powder, 174
Powers, 15
Prosperity
    Money Charm Bag, 188
    Prosperity Meditation Spell, 71–72
    Prosperity Tea, 143
Protection
    Protection Powder, 173
    Protection Salve, 170
    Protection Tea, 143
    Winter Protection Spell: A Witch's Bottle, 79–81
Psychic powers, 181

R

Rhiannon, 14
Rose geranium, 28
Runes, 25

S

Sabbats, 35–36. *See also specific*
Salves, 167
    Protection Salve, 170
    Rosebud Love Salve, 169
    Wiccan Dream Salve, 167–168

Samhain, 36
    Samhain Candles, 192
    Samhain Incense, 175
    Samhain Sabbat Oil, 159
    Samhain Sabbat Ritual, 86–87
    Samhain Soul Cakes, 120–121
Seasons
    Autumn Count Your Blessings Spell, 77–78
    Early Spring Spell of Hope, 73–74
    Summer Spell of Courage, 75–76
    Winter Protection Spell: A Witch's Bottle, 79–81
Self-dedication, 18–20
September Harvest Moon, 39
Smudging, 201
Solitary Wicca, 3–4, 21, 205
Suburban Wiccans, 5

T

Tarot cards, 25
Teas, 139
    Attract Love Tea, 139
    Banishing Tea, 140
    Courage Tea, 140
    Divination Tea, 141
    Happiness Tea, 142
    Healing Tea, 141
    Lucky Tea, 143
    Protection Tea, 143
Threefold Law, 7
Tools, 24–25
Turning of the Wheel, 33

U

Urban Wiccans, 6

V

Vervain, 26

W

Wands, 25
Water element, 17
    Element of Water Potion, 199
Wheel of the Year, 33
Wicca, history of, 2
Witchcraft Today (Gardner), 2
Witch's Pyramid, 104–105

Y

Yule, 35
    Yule Candles, 192
    Yule Gingerbread Magick Charm Cookies, 122–124
    Yule Incense, 175
    Yule Sabbat Oil, 160
    Yule Sabbat Ritual, 88–90

ACKNOWLEDGMENTS

First, I would like to thank Callisto Media for seeking me out and allowing me to write this book, and I would also like to thank Jesse Aylen, who edited it.

I'm grateful to my husband, Duane, who is always there for me with support and love.

To Jesse and Laure, I am in awe of your accomplishments. You're who I want to be when I grow up!

To my coven sisters, we walk the Wiccan Path together in love and light. You teach me so much every time we meet; I can't imagine life without you.

To my friends, you know who you are; I thank you for your love and acceptance, weekend getaways, island retreats, games night, and way too much good food.

ABOUT THE AUTHOR

Rowan Morgana has been a Wiccan priestess and coven sister for more than 20 years. She is a crone and craft elder who specializes in writing spells and rituals. She is married and has a grown son and daughter-in-law currently living in Australia. Rowan Morgana is well known online through her website at SacredWicca.com, Etsy shop Morgana Magick Spell, and social media. Besides practicing witchcraft, Rowan also loves being out in her large garden, camping with her husband, hanging with her besties, playing board games, walking in nature with her faithful hounds, and going on the yearly "girl cruise."

www.ingramcontent.com/pod-product-compliance
Lightning Source LLC
Chambersburg PA
CBHW041927090426
42743CB00021B/3460